All the Company of Heaven

Dr Kenneth Stevenson is the Bishop of Portsmouth and a member of the Doctrine Commission of the Church of England. A leading Anglican scholar, he is the author of numerous books including *Covenant of Grace Renewed* (DLT), *The Mystery of Baptism* (Canterbury Press Norwich) and *The Mystery of the Eucharist* (co-authored with H. R. McAdoo and also published by the Canterbury Press Norwich).

All the Company of Heaven

A companion to the principal festivals of the Christian year

Kenneth Stevenson

CANTERBURY
PRESS

Norwich

© Kenneth Stevenson 1998

First published in 1998 by The Canterbury Press Norwich
(a publishing imprint of Hymns Ancient & Modern Limited
a registered charity)
St Mary's Works, St Mary's Plain
Norwich, Norfolk, NR3 3BH

British Library Cataloguing in Publication Data

A catalogue record for this book is available
from the British Library

ISBN 1-85311-217-8

Typeset by Rowland Phototypesetting,
Bury St Edmunds, Suffolk
Printed in Great Britain by
Biddles Ltd, Guildford and King's Lynn

Contents

Preface

When I was a boy, I used to be an altar server during school holidays at our one weekday Eucharist which was on Thursday morning. I always looked forward to those occasions when the Thursday coincided with a saint's or holy day, because this meant that we had a change from the Collect and readings for the previous Sunday. I suppose this regular experience built in me an unconscious love of the calendar, which meant that much later on when I had to preach sermons, I took delight in exploiting its riches just now and again. I can remember on one occasion preaching to a small gathering of people who braved the winter snow to come to Evensong on the Sunday after Christmas. They were rewarded for their labours by having to listen to me not only on Saint Stephen, but Saint John the Evangelist and the Holy Innocents as well!

When the invitation came to write this book, I made the decision that for each occasion there should be four main ingredients: an exploration of the meaning of the person or the festival; some background history about its evolution; a discussion of the readings associated with the day, and the prayers; and finally, a quotation from a recognized Anglican author.

There are many friends who deserve my thanks. I want to thank Andrew Davis, my chaplain, for his theological friendship, and Edmund Ivens, the priest who nurtured me from my childhood, who died shortly after this book was completed. I owe a great debt of gratitude, too, to Michael Adie, who across the years has always been a model of distilled learning and holy 'common sense'. I must also thank Martin Kitchen, for his wise comments on the use of the Bible. David Price's organ-playing in the Cathedral proved an inspiration at a critical stage. These pages have emerged from a book-filled study with two sleeping border terriers silently encouraging me, and also from a chapel dedicated to All Saints, which has provided another dimension of nourishment. Kitty Price and Julie Anderson have readily devoured the material handed them and provided a clean type-script. Sarah, my wife, has always been an encouragement, and to her this book is dedicated, with love.

Kenneth Stevenson
Bishopsgrove
Fareham

Feast of the Presentation
of Christ in the Temple, 1998

Prologue
Whose Company?

'The whole company of heaven' is a phrase which resonates. It suggests many images and in particular sums up the purpose of this book, which is to explore the work of Christ in the great celebrations of the Calendar and the Church Year, and to see how he triumphs in the lives of the New Testament saints. For the communion of saints is not an idea to which some people may or may not give assent. It is a great truth of the Christian faith, a present reality, which transcends even that occasional sense of the numinous which may impact upon a chance visitor to an ancient building. The word 'company' suggests sharing the same meal, as the Latin word *panis* (bread) implies, and that meal is the eucharistic banquet which is set for all of us – now.

But this great truth is found not just in the high-flown language of the Christian tradition. It can be discerned in the ways in which ordinary imperfect lives became touched in different ways by Christ himself: how his life took root in Galilean fishermen, in a devout Pharisee named Saul who at first hated the followers of the preacher from Nazareth, and in countless women and men ever since. The 'communion of saints' is not a select club for initiates who talk with the correct accent and exchange semaphore signals to each other. It is a fellowship, a company, in which there are always going to be more members, more ways of following Christ, more truths of God to celebrate.

This is one of the reasons why 'the whole company of heaven' holds such a fascination. There are favourites for some, either because their lives express something of our struggles, like hot-tempered, impulsive Peter denying Christ three times, only to become the leader of the apostolic band; or because they are the exact opposite of our particular walk of faith, like Philip, who had the imagination to point out at the crisis-conference before the feeding of the five thousand that there was a lad here with five small loaves and two pickled fish, but what was that among so many . . . ? Then there are the 'patron' saints, like Andrew, who according to an old legend had his relics brought to St Andrews, and became associated with Scotland; or Jude, about whom we know so little that he is the patron saint of lost causes.

These names, and many others besides, become very much part of the life of a bishop, because every day particular parishes appear in the cycle of prayer with their dedications – which may have been chosen for reasons that are obvious as well as baffling. The church in the parish in which this book was written is dedicated to St Peter and St Paul, a very popular combination in the Middle Ages, symbolizing the unity of the missionary enterprise in the early Church in two quite different personalities. To select a dedication, like all selections, means excluding other possibilities. Let me give an example of my own.

During the early part of 1997, it became clear that a choice would have to be made for the new chapel in the new bishop's house, to which we were due to move in the autumn. Because all these dedications began to mean so much to me, the decision was taken to dedicate the chapel to All Saints, a major feast to which I have always been particularly attached. I suppose the reasons were partly the paintings of the saints themselves, partly the beautiful hymns and music associated with the day, and partly because the beginning of the Sermon on the Mount – the gospel for 1 November – has sometimes been described, with some poetic licence, as the greatest sermon ever preached.

Then the question was raised – what sort of decor would be appropriate? For reasons of economy and the need for simplicity in a comparatively small space with lots of woodwork, we needed something bold. Eventually we looked eastward – and hit on the idea of an icon by Dom Anselm Shobrook of the

Anglican Benedictine Community at Alton. The icon radiates prayerfulness and beauty by its gold-leafed background and its three figures, Christ, the Virgin Mary and John the Baptist. In the centre sits Christ on a throne, his right hand raised in blessing, his left hand holding a book in which is inscribed the first and the last letters of the Greek alphabet, alpha and omega, the two letters with which Christ describes himself at the beginning and end of the last book of the Bible, the Revelation of St John.

But what of the other two figures? Both look towards Christ and are incomplete without him. Saints are not supposed to get in the way of the relationship between Christ and his people! But Mary and John the Baptist are different. John's bearing is tense, his face and arms are taut, and he stretches towards Jesus as the 'forerunner', always pointing beyond himself. He knows life to be unsatisfactory – and he has the courage to say so. But he is waiting for someone else – not himself – somehow to put things right. Mary, on the other hand, is a calmer and more fulfilled figure. She is not the glossy young mother of the first Christmas Day, but has the haggard complexion of Easter maturity. She is the 'bearer of God', the one who brought Christ into the world. She too knows life to be unsatisfactory, but she sees its questions in sharper relief, where love that costs is the throbbing heart of divine reality.

The experience of 'the whole of the company of heaven' is that we have to live with both the frustration of being the Lord's forerunner, and the fulfilment (however partial) of bearing him in the world. The life of faith is neither about waiting for something to happen, nor about frenzied activity to ensure that the pet scheme is implemented exactly according to the original plan – and on schedule as well. The saints had to live with contradictions, and that is why they are all marked with the sign of the cross.

In the same way that a dedication is an act of selection, so are the contents of this book. We shall confine ourselves to Principal Feasts and Festivals and Principal Holy Days of the Church of England, as now authorized, which are approximately those in the rest of the Anglican Communion. The dates of the principal holy days necessarily vary from year to year; they provide the essential foundation for the work of redemption which produced the saints in the first place, namely Ash Wednesday, Palm Sunday, Maundy Thursday, Good Friday, Easter Day, Ascension Day, Pentecost and Trinity Sunday. Some of these occasions date from the earliest times – like Easter Day, *the* feast of all feasts. Others, like the Naming of Jesus, are (surprisingly) less ancient. Biblical background often comes into play. For example, whereas Luke provides the basis for the festivals involving the Virgin Mary and gives the fullest account of John the Baptist, Matthew gives us a clearer portrait of Joseph, the wise men of the Epiphany and the Holy Innocents. And whereas it is John's Gospel which develops the characters of Philip, Mary Magdalene and Thomas, it is the Acts of the Apostles which gives evidence for Matthias, Stephen, the Conversion of St Paul, Barnabas, and James the Great.

The icon which I have described evokes many prayers. These include the Collects for each occasion, some of which go back many centuries, as well as the (optional) Post-Communion Prayers, which are mostly recent compositions, but are nonetheless rich in the eucharistic imagery of sacramental feeding, faithful discipleship, and the life of heaven. There are, indeed, times when the icon itself suggests more than the three figures of Christ, the Virgin Mary and John the Baptist. Indeed, it seems to go all the way round the chapel, with icons of any number of saints and church dedications, to embrace and inspire every worshipper; for we are all, potentially, part of the whole company of heaven.

Such is the quest which the human race was always intended to pursue, and it is a noble though by no means an easy one. At the end of a series of sermons on the Lord's Prayer preached in the spring of 1848, when Europe was gripped by revolutions and social and political life was shot through with anxiety as much as with hope, F. D. Maurice (1805–72) directed his hearers to the very centre of Christian prayer, and that same hope to which we are all called:

> . . . what we desire for ourselves and for our race – the greatest redemption we can dream of – is gathered up in the words, 'Thine is the glory.' Self-willing, self-seeking, self-glorifying, here is the curse: no shackles remain when these are gone; nothing can be wanting when the spirit sees itself, loses itself, in Him who is Light, and in whom is no darkness at all. In these words therefore we see the ground and consummation of our prayer; they shew how prayer begins and ends in Sacrifice and Adoration. They teach us how Prayer, which we might fancy was derived from the wants of an imperfect, suffering creature, belongs equally to the redeemed and perfected. In these the craving for independence has ceased; they are content to ask and to receive. But their desire of knowledge and love never ceases. They have awaked up after His likeness, and are satisfied with it; but the thought, 'Thine is the glory,' opens to them a vision which must become wider and brighter for ever and ever. Amen.

F. D. Maurice, *The Lord's Prayer – Nine Sermons Preached in the Chapel of Lincoln's Inn* (Cambridge: Macmillan, 1861), p. 130.

Part One: The Calendar

The Naming and Circumcision of Jesus

1 January (Festival – White or Gold)

The beginning of a new year is – on the surface – the mere passing of one day into another. But it has long had special associations. Measuring time goes back far longer than our best documentary evidence, and like all measurements it is subdivided accordingly. A full day marks the rotation of the earth on its axis. A full year marks the revolution of the earth round the sun. Every four years an intercalated day at the end of February makes up for lost time. It was the ancient Romans who decided that the year should begin on 1 January – *Ianua* means a door, the door to the next year. And although many people still regard the year as starting on 1 January, the academic year usually begins in the autumn, like the civil year in the Byzantine Empire.

The Christian Year could be said to begin in perhaps three different places. The season of Advent marks a fresh start, when the imagination is kindled to look forward to the coming of Christ, specifically at Christmas itself. But Easter is the most ancient festival of all, the origin of the Christian faith, the day on which God raised Christ from the dead. Still, we have to begin somewhere, and 1 January is as good as any time, because however 'religious' we make our celebrations, the message of the Christian faith is that it is about God entering into and redeeming the human race, and therefore no human experience that is of any importance can be ignored.

The beginning of the secular year is also associated with new resolutions. It would be interesting to know exactly how many of these actually work! But whatever the success – or lack of it – the very fact that people have attempted such ideals about

themselves suggests that an important passage of time should
be marked by placing ourselves under some kind of spiritual
microscope. How are we – in the broadest terms? Are we becoming, in any way, better people? Or is it just a case of stumbling
along, and getting up again, as one of the Desert Fathers suggested? The answer is partly given by recourse to the fundamental truths that nature and grace work together, and that the grace
of God is often concealed in the lives that we lead. Therefore we
look to Christ, the source of that grace.

This may be why it is something of a delightful coincidence
that 1 January follows seven days after 25 December, the feast
of the Nativity of Christ. For on the eighth day, newborn males
are circumcised and named, according to Jewish practice. As
we shall see, each of the four Gospel writers has a particular
perspective on the life of Christ; and surrounding the early life
of Jesus, it is Matthew and Luke who give us important details.
Both tell us that the baby born to Mary was to be called Jesus,
a common name meaning 'saviour'. In Matthew it was revealed
in the dream which Joseph had (Matt. 1:21), whereas in Luke
it was the angel speaking directly to Mary (Luke 1:31). But
Luke is the writer who actually recounts Jesus being circumcised
and named on the eighth day after his birth (Luke 2:15–21 –
the gospel for today).

For the early Christians, the *name* of Jesus held a special
significance. We all know that names mean different things.
Sarah means 'princess' and Kenneth means 'leader'. For the Son
of Mary, conceived by the Holy Spirit, to be called Jesus is more
than just a name. In Jewish tradition, names expressed aspects
of personality. That his naming and circumcision took place in
the Temple is important for Christians because it roots Jesus in
historical fact, and prevents him from flitting into some vague
religious experience. That he was circumcised indicates that he
entered a tradition, and shed blood, as he was to do uniquely
on the cross. His name permeated his ministry to the extent that
miracles were performed in the name of Jesus (Mark 9:38ff.;
Acts 4:30); baptism is performed in the name of Jesus (Acts

2:38); we are justified through the name of Jesus (1 Cor. 6:11); so that Jesus is the name above all others (Phil. 2:9ff.). It becomes, therefore, impossible to separate the Christian faith from the name of Jesus. All Christian prayer is through 'Jesus Christ our Lord'. This is not only a liturgical convention to indicate that the prayer is drawing to an end, but a statement that all prayer is offered in the power of the Spirit, and in union with Christ, in heaven.

It was not until the later Middle Ages that a feast of the Holy Name was gradually included in the calendars of the Western Church. It was popular among the Franciscans, to whom is attributed the 'Litany of the Holy Name' in the fifteenth century. Various dates were adopted, 14 January or – as in medieval England – 7 August, in order to focus exclusively on this mystery, thus leaving 1 January to commemorate the Circumcision. After the Second Vatican Council, the Roman Catholic Church reverted to a much older custom of celebrating Mary the Mother of God on 1 January, a commemoration that antedates the Marian feasts, some of which we shall encounter in due course. But contemporary Anglican practice is – to put it at its most direct – to follow Scripture, and on the eighth day after the Nativity to celebrate what Luke recounts and its consequences for us.

The Collect for today is based on the 1662 Prayer Book, which is in turn adapted from a much older form found in the Gregorian Sacramentary, the book of prayers representing Roman practice from the seventh century. It begins by mentioning Christ's obedient circumcision, and then meditates on his name and the faithful missionary imperative that ensues. The Old Testament reading (Num. 6:22–7) is the so-called Aaronic Blessing ('The Lord bless you and keep you'), which is the means by which they shall 'put my name upon the people of Israel, and I will bless them' (Num. 6:27). The epistle (Gal. 4:4–7) concentrates on our adoption as children of God. Both of these readings lead suitably into the account given by Luke of the shepherds going to the manger, their departure, and Christ's first visit to the Temple for his naming and circumcision (Luke 2:15–21). The Post-Communion Prayer is a new composition, which rejoices in the sacramental feeding at Christ's table, and prays that we 'may live out our years in the power of the Name above all other names', a happy allusion to the calendar's new start. Everything is drawn together but the challenge of the future is far from denied.

Jesus' name continues to fascinate and inspire, and to draw us towards a view of salvation which never stops, as Peter Selby (1941–   ) states:

> Jesus is Saviour. So he is called and so, in the faith of Christians, he turned out to be. For the people of Jesus' world, it could be no surprise that persons could turn out as their name suggests; that was in a way only to be expected. Behind the naming of Jesus lies a long tradition that attaches a great significance to the names people have, especially if they are the names which God gives them.

> Peter Selby, *Rescue: Jesus and Salvation Today* (London: SPCK, 1995), p. 16.

The Epiphany

6 January (Principal Feast – White or Gold)

I once went to a school Nativity Play, at which all the traditional
ingredients were present. Mary and Joseph, the donkey, no room
at the inn in Bethlehem, shepherds abiding in the fields – and
wise men from the east. When the wise men made their first
appearance on stage, one of their number halted, pointed firmly
and dramatically towards the ceiling of the school assembly hall,
and said, 'Look at that bright star in the sky. It tells us that a
king has been born. Let us follow it and see.'

The wise men from the east have fed artists and poets across
the centuries. Perhaps one of the most famous is T. S. Eliot's
'Journey of the Magi', a poem first published in 1927, which
begins with a more retrospective view than the one uttered by
that small schoolboy:

> A cold coming we had of it,
> Just the worst time of the year
> For a journey, and such a long journey;
> The ways deep and the weather sharp,
> The very dead of winter.

Eliot was clearly gripped by the entire idea of the wise men
coming from the east to Jerusalem (Matt. 2:1–12), for it suggested to him a journey that was more than physical, and was
ultimately about faith. He had been inspired to write this poem
by his reading of the sermon preached by Lancelot Andrewes
(1555–1626) on Christmas Day 1622 at Whitehall, before King

James. Even the poem's repeated mannerisms – 'set down this' – suggest the understandable impatience of enthusiasm that wants to tell the whole story from the heart and from the mind.

We do not know who these wise men were supposed to be. 'Magi' (as Matthew calls them) were an ancient caste of a priestly kind from Persia. At the time of Jesus, some magi were known for their scientific knowledge whereas others were more like magicians. Perhaps Matthew intends both a scientific and religious slant to this journey 'from the east'. But he does not mention any number – and it was not until the third century that Tertullian refers to them as kings and Origen assumes that there were three of them to correspond with their gifts. Matthew – the most obviously Jewish of the four Gospel writers – appropriately brings those who are outside the Jewish faith into the Bethlehem scene before anyone else. They have to do so in an atmosphere of political tension. When the compilers of the 1662 Prayer Book added 'the manifestation of Christ to the Gentiles' as a subtitle they were following a long tradition in the West that associated Epiphany almost exclusively with the wise men. There was clearly more than enough to ponder, including wrestling with the interpretation of those gifts. These were gifts that only wealthy people could bring. Later Christian interpretation portrays gold as a symbol of wisdom and wealth, incense as a symbol of worship and sacrifice, and myrrh as a symbol of healing – and even embalming. Jesus was going to challenge and set aright the way in which the world handled all three.

But Epiphany was – and is – about far more than this particular episode and its subsequent developments in piety and art. In the Eastern Orthodox Church, and throughout the Byzantine Rite, today is called 'Theophany'. This is a sharper title. 'Epiphany' means manifesting forth, whereas 'Theophany' means manifesting *God*. And, as if to pile on the different ways in which God was shown forth at the start of Christ's ministry, this festival celebrated not only the wise men coming from the east (Matt. 2:1–12), but the baptism of Christ in the Jordan (recounted in the Gospels) and Christ turning water into wine at the wedding in Cana (John 2:1–11). This is the great theme in most of the Eastern Churches, the Coptic and the Syrian as well as the Byzantine. Relics of it are to be found in the West in the older service books of the Middle Ages. Modern revisions – including *The Promise of His Glory* (1991) – find eloquent expression in the liturgical statement, 'Three wonders mark this Holy Day.'

For many people, however, the wise men are enough. The Baptism of Christ can be celebrated on the Sunday after, and Jesus at Cana on the Sunday following. The 'Epiphanies' start at Bethlehem and go on and on right through Christ's ministry, as Christopher Wordsworth (1807–85) suggests in his hymn 'Songs of thankfulness and praise', whose first three stanzas are as follows:

> Songs of thankfulness and praise,
> Jesu, Lord, to thee we raise,
> Manifested by the star
> To the sages from afar;
> Branch of royal David's stem
> In thy birth at Bethlehem:
> Anthems be to thee addrest,
> God in Man made manifest.
>
> Manifest at Jordan's stream,
> Prophet, Priest, and King supreme;
> And at Cana wedding-guest
> In thy Godhead manifest;
> Manifest in power divine,
> Changing water into wine:
> Anthems be to thee addrest,
> God in Man made manifest.
>
> Manifest in making whole
> Palsied limbs and fainting soul;

Manifest in valiant fight,
Quelling all the devil's might;
Manifest in gracious will,
Ever bringing good from ill:
Anthems be to thee addrest,
God in Man made manifest.

(*Hymns Ancient and Modern New Standard*, no. 53)

We cannot, of course, expect a uniform picture of how 'Epiphany' in its broadest sense is celebrated across the Christian spectrum. In fact, Eastern and Western Christians are almost equally divided by the emphasis they place on 25 December as the Nativity of Christ, and 6 January as the 'Theophany' of Christ. Both feasts are kept, with slightly different nuances, in all traditions. But why those dates? Two theories have been advanced. One is that as the Christian Church began to emerge from a time of persecution in the fourth century, there was the need to 'Christianize' the older pagan commemorations of the Midwinter Solstice, which in the West was on 25 December and in the East was on 6 January. Another and more subtle view relates these two celebrations back nine months to 25 March and 6 April respectively, as two dates in ancient calendars for the death of Christ and also his conception. In order to see his life whole, some early Christians were keen to identify the beginning and end as having taken place on the same day, in much the same way that Jewish tradition sometimes maintained that the world was created on the same day of the year as the Passover. These two interpretations, perhaps, indicate two different approaches to the way the Christian life should be worked out. One conquers by Christianization, whereas the other creeps slowly in and absorbs.

And what of those other Epiphany themes? We know that there was a blessing of water on this day in Egypt at the time of Clement of Alexandria in the third century. This could be a sign of antiquity, and the magi (Matt. 2:1–12) and Cana (John

2:1–11) were simply added. It is even possible that favourite Gospel writers at this solemn season were read in the great centres associated with them; Matthew in Jerusalem, John in Ephesus, and Mark in Alexandria. We can also note that Mark's Gospel has no infancy narratives whatever, and simply begins with the preaching of John the Baptist and the baptism of Jesus. Whatever the truth behind these details, it is important to note the link between Epiphany and baptism – which is so important in iconography in both East and West.

The Collect for today stresses the 'manifestation' of Christ. It is based on that of the Prayer Book, which is in turn taken from that which appears in the Roman Gregorian Sacramentary. The star leads us to Christ, through whom we hope to reach heaven. The Old Testament lesson (Isa. 60:1–6) is a vision of a light that shines over the darkness of the earth and draws all nations to the Lord; it was the lesson for the epistle in the Middle Ages. The epistle reading, on the other hand, dates from the Prayer Book, and draws the Gentiles into the Christian faith, and has the beauty of doing so in a way that cannot be interpreted as anti-semitic (Eph. 3:1–12). The gospel tells the story of the magi coming to Bethlehem, guided by the star (Matt. 2:1–12). The Post-Communion Prayer, a new composition, comes from *The Promise of His Glory* (1991); the worshipper walks with the wise men to the manifested Christ and asks for grace to discern that glory in the future.

This same truth lies behind a passage from a sermon preached by Edward Talbot (1844–1934) in Leeds Parish Church on 'The duty of shining':

> We are, each of us, but a lamp. The light is what God gave thee, who lighted a conscience within thee, and made thee able to love, and to be brave, and true, and pure. The light is what Christ has brought thee. It is called *thy* light, indeed, in his kindness because he trusted it to thee; but it is not thine own. It is his through thee; hindered by thy fault, dimmed

by thy dullness. His is its native purity, and thine only by his
grant, so long as thou art true to him.

Edward Talbot, *Sermons Preached in Leeds Parish Church* (London:
Rivingtons, 1896), pp. 89ff.

The Baptism of Christ

(Principal Holy Day – White)

Organ music holds a much-valued place in Christian worship, especially in the Lutheran tradition, where each hymn is often introduced and concluded by a brilliant improvisation on its melody and mood. J. S. Bach (1685–1750) was particularly adept at this art, and his 'Chorale Preludes' are among the most intriguing of his compositions. One particular example is the prelude on the Epiphany hymn by Martin Luther himself (1483–1546), 'Christ, unser Herr, zum Jordan kam' (To Jordan came the Christ our Lord).

The melody is played at medium pitch on the pedal and is easily identifiable in all its firmness because it is not embellished in any way. The manual parts, however, form something of a contrast. The left hand flows up and down the scale of C minor in a repeated motif that suggests flowing water. The right hand, however, dances through the principal gaps in the octaves (playing an arpeggio), which suggests descent from above. The three parts play together, a bold but intricate unity, yet retain their identity. Bach, the devout Lutheran, had pondered long the full meaning of this beloved hymn, particularly the fourth verse:

> There stood the Son of God in love,
> His grace to us extending;
> The Holy Spirit like a dove
> Upon the scene descending;
> The triune God assuring us,
> With promises compelling

That in our baptism he will thus
Among us find a dwelling.
To comfort and sustain us.

The baptism of Christ has long been interpreted in Trinitarian terms: the Father speaking to Christ in the voice (the strong melody in the pedal); Jesus himself in the water (the flowing motif); the Spirit in the dove hovering over him (the dancing right hand motif). Such an interpretation has a long history in East and West, and it was explored in the seventeenth century by Lancelot Andrewes (1555–1626), Jeremy Taylor (1613–67) and Herbert Thorndike (1598–1672). The Christian is drawn into Christ's own baptism in Christ's act of redemption, through the work of the Holy Spirit, for to be baptized is to be drawn into the divine life itself (see Trinity Sunday).

This truth Luther boldly grasped. He wrote the hymn for Epiphany, a feast for which he preferred the gospel passage to be Matthew's account of the baptism of Christ (Matt. 3:13–17). He did so in the face of its more popular association with the wise men (Matt. 2:1–12), which had already given rise to the Nordic nickname 'Holy Three Kings Day'. In doing so, he was looking to the Eastern tradition, which, as we have seen, draws together the baptism, the wise men, and Christ at Cana. More specifically, Luther may well have been inspired by the practice of the Greek Orthodox Church, and the whole Byzantine rite, of keeping 7 January (the day after Epiphany) as a celebration of John the Baptist, at which the retrospective narrative of Christ's baptism as recorded in the Fourth Gospel is appointed to be read (John 1:29–34). Nor was he entirely out of step with the West, for there are a few early medieval lectionaries which direct the narrative of Christ's baptism as it appears in one or other of the first three Gospels to be read as the gospel passage on a day following Epiphany. But this custom never really caught on, and reads like an unsuccessful experiment. Uniquely, the Danish Church after the Lutheran Reformation retained Epiphany as the feast of the three Kings, but made the

Sunday before Lent a commemoration of the baptism (Matt. 3:13–17) as the immediate prelude to Christ's journey into the wilderness for forty day (Matt. 4:1–11).

The baptism of Christ never entirely budges! For example, in the Scottish *Book of Common Prayer* (1929), there is an optional Post-Communion Prayer originally written by John Dowden (1840–1910) for Epiphany and the seven days after, which links the baptism of Christ closely to the manifestation of 'his glorious god-head', and goes on to pray 'that the brightness of his presence may shine in our hearts, and his glory be set forth in our lives'. (This prayer also appears in *The Promise of His Glory* (1991)). Such sentiments as these were a harbinger of the renewal of baptismal faith and practice that has taken place in so many of the Churches in recent years. After the Second Vatican Council, the Sunday after Epiphany in the Roman scheme became the Feast of the Baptism of Christ. This was in effect drawing together the medieval experiment noted earlier, Eastern liturgical practice, and Luther's teaching, and building from them something eminently appropriate for an era of baptismal renewal. Clearly, there is a significant baptismal 'memory' at Epiphany that was lying ready to be taken out into the light of day. The new provisions, therefore, do precisely this, and they were in any case anticipated in part by *The Alternative Service Book (1980)*, from which today's Collect is taken. Like Luther's hymn and Bach's Chorale Prelude, it is both Trinitarian and baptismal. It begins in Trinitarian style: 'Eternal Father, who at the baptism of Jesus revealed him to be your Son, anointing him with the Holy Spirit'. And it continues by drawing us into the baptismal life: 'Grant to us, who were born again by water in the Spirit, that we may be faithful to our calling as your adopted children.'

The readings follow the three-year cycle. Year A takes us through the servant called by God (Isa. 42:1–9) and Peter's speech that mentions Christ's baptism, where he was anointed with the Holy Spirit and 'with power' (Acts 10:34–43), to Matthew's account of the baptism of Christ (Matt. 3:13–17).

Matthew's narrative includes John's initial reluctance to baptize Jesus, and it ends with the voice saying, 'This is my beloved Son, with whom I am well pleased.'

Year B, on the other hand, starts with the very beginning of the Old Testament, the first day of creation, and the creation of light (Gen. 1:1–5); it goes on to Peter baptizing those who had only heard of John's baptism at Corinth (Acts 19:1–7); and Mark's narrative of Christ's baptism is the gospel (Mark 1:4–11). John's appearance and his preaching are described; Jesus' baptism follows, and – unlike in Matthew – the voice from heaven addresses Christ directly, '*Thou* art my beloved Son; with thee I am well pleased.'

In Year C, we read of the promise of God's presence through the waters, which will not overwhelm us, created for God's glory (Isa. 43:1–7); the second reading tells of the Spirit falling on the Samaritans, thanks to Peter and John's ministry (Acts 8:14–17); and the gospel is Luke's narrative of Christ's baptism (Luke 3:15–17, 21–2). It is more retrospective than the other two, though not as retrospective as the Fourth Gospel. (This does not come across so clearly when – as here – verses 18–20 are omitted, since these tell of Herod's arrest of John the Baptist.) When it comes to the baptism itself, Luke takes care to mention that all the people are present, that Jesus prays, and that the Spirit comes upon him in bodily form. In other words, baptism is public; prayer (a significant feature of Jesus' life in Luke's Gospel) is an essential part; and the Spirit's presence is an *embodiment* of God himself. Luke follows Mark as the voice addresses Christ directly: 'Thou art my beloved Son; with thee I am well pleased.' The Post-Communion Prayer, a new composition, echoes the theme of the Collect, namely the revelation of the Trinity ('you opened the heavens and revealed yourself as Father . . .') and prays for the continued presence of God in our lives ('complete the heavenly work of our rebirth through the waters of the new creation').

The repertoire of baptismal prayers shows no signs of abating. This is to be heartily welcomed, because it shows that the font is being taken more seriously now than for many years. Baptism is both an event and a process, as Jesus' own life and ministry manifests: from the Jordan, he went into the wilderness, and thereafter his ministry began. Baptism, therefore, is the beginning and not the result, and a Church that is rediscovering its riches can run the risk of trying to make people ready, instead of proclaiming baptism as the sacrament of God's invitation to us. Geoffrey Lampe (1912–80) articulates this truth in the following way:

Baptism signifies God's creative and saving grace, the outreach of his love to his rational creatures ... The initiative in conversion and in all that baptism signifies lies with God. Faith, from its most rudimentary beginnings onwards, is a movement of God the Spirit in man. The human 'decision' is no more than the natural and proper response of God's creature to the outgoing love of the Creator in whom he already has his being and who already dwells in him.

Baptism is necessarily a sacrament of promise because it is an initiation, standing at the very beginning of Christian life. It does, certainly, signify the whole gospel and man's whole response to the gospel, but its meaning has to be unfolded progressively as time goes on, and the rite itself is only the initial moment of that developing process.

G. W. H. Lampe, *God As Spirit: the Bampton Lectures 1976* (Oxford: Clarendon Press, 1977), p. 190.

The Conversion of St Paul

25 January (Festival – White)

It is sometimes said that repetition is the sign of a good story-line. 'Tell me the old, old story' is a hymn that suggests exactly that truth. To repeat something does not necessarily imply that the hearers are deaf, though that may be the case. But it can suggest that the truth is so fundamental that it lies somewhere between the words that were used.

Repetition does indeed lie at the heart of today's celebration, for the Conversion of St Paul is narrated no fewer than three times in the Acts of the Apostles. No other event in a person's life is given treatment on this scale in the New Testament, apart (of course) from Jesus. First of all, there is the narrative of Paul's conversion in the sequence of events in the first part of the Acts of the Apostles (Acts 9:1–22). Then, towards the end, Paul himself gives his own account, first in a speech in Hebrew to the crowd in Jerusalem after his arrest (Acts 22:6–16) and afterwards in Greek in the more private context before the Governor Festus and King Agrippa (Acts 16:12–18).

There must be a significance behind this repetition. First comes the narrative; then a speech in Hebrew to the Jewish public, then a speech in Greek to the powers that be. Narrative followed by public harangue followed by semi-public discourse provide the living and costly context in which Christianity was born. Here is Saul of Tarsus, a Pharisee who condoned the stoning of Stephen, who was converted on the road to Damascus where he intended to persecute the Christians, and who thereafter became zealous with his Christian faith, as his actions and words demonstrated. His actions bore witness in the three great missionary journeys to Cyprus, to Asia Minor and Eastern Greece, and to Ephesus, Macedonia and Achaea (Acts 13:1–14:28; 15:30–21:16). On those journeys he risked being beaten up, arrested and maltreated, and he had to invoke being a Roman citizen in order to ensure that his case was heard before the Emperor (Acts 25:11).

His words were born out of that experience. Redemption is through faith in Christ (Rom. 3:21–6). Jesus is the eternal, pre-existing Son of the Father (Phil. 2:5–11). The Church is the mystical body of Christ (Col. 1:15–20). The believer is baptized into Christ's death and and resurrection (Rom. 6:3–11). According to early tradition, Paul was a small, bald, bandy-legged man, with a long nose, eyebrows meeting – features which give every indication of the intensity with which his personality is reflected in so many pages of the New Testament. Here is a man whose writings have influenced theologians across the centuries, including Augustine, Luther and Calvin.

It is possible, of course, that in the narrative and the two speeches that recount his conversion (each has its particular features), we have something of a retrospective view of the conversion of Paul of Tarsus. After all, the Acts of the Apostles was written by Luke as a mild form of early Christian propaganda, in order to combat the charge that Christians were disloyal to the Roman Empire, and that it was both possible and reasonable – as well as divinely intended – that people should become Christians. The wise men coming from the east to Jerusalem is a Matthean scene. Like the Naming and Circumcision of Christ, the Conversion of Paul is a Lucan one.

Perhaps it was the *repetition* of Paul's conversion that gave rise to the special character of this festival. As we shall see, Peter and Paul were originally commemorated – together – on 29 June, and in most traditions they still are. We first encounter provision for today at the end of the sixth century in France, in the so-called Gothic Missal, a book which has many features that indicate a somewhat different liturgical temperament from the more austere rites in use in Rome and elsewhere. In the latter part of the eighth century, the feast reappears in the Sacramentaries (books of prayers for the sacraments), and it was inevitable that it would survive the Reformation in England, not least because of the prominent place given to Paul's theology by the Reformers.

The Collect is based on that of the Prayer Book, which in turn is based on the medieval Latin prayer used on this day. As far as the readings are concerned, there is an element of choice. The narrative of Paul's conversion (Acts 9:1–22) has always been read. It can be read either first instead of the Old Testament reading, or second, if an Old Testament reading is to be used. The prophecy of Jeremiah begins by asserting that Jeremiah has been called by God from the womb – a very Pauline theme (Jer. 1:4–10). The epistle alludes to Paul's conversion (Gal. 1:11–16a); perhaps a more suitable reading here might have been found in one of the classic Pauline expositions of justification by faith, e.g. Romans 3:21–6. The gospel reading has been long associated with today; we are called to leave everything behind, and the first should be last and the last first (Matt. 19:27–30). The Post-Communion Prayer provides us with a choice. The first prays for boldness to preach the gospel, and is the alternative collect for Pentecost in *The Alternative Service Book (1980)*. The second prays for fidelity to 'the apostles' teaching and fellowship' (Acts 2:42) and is from the Canadian *Book of Alternative Services* (1985). We shall meet this provision again on festivals of apostles and evangelists.

Paul always leaves us wrestling with the contrast between what we leave behind and what we look forward to. Such a truth is well summed up by Peter Baelz (1923-):

> In the seminal thought of St Paul we find there are recurring tensions between salvation as a present reality and as a future hope, between the proclamation of the gospel of forgiveness and the summons to realise to their full extent the implications for life and behaviour for this newly established

divine–human relationship. Believers are to become what they already are. Born of the Spirit they are to walk by the Spirit.

Peter Baelz, *Prayer and Providence* (London: SCM Press, 1968), p. 89.

The Presentation of Christ in the Temple

2 February (Principal Feast – White or Gold)

There is a Rembrandt painting of the Presentation in the Temple which dates from about 1628. The aged Simeon is seated, holding the baby Jesus in his left arm, and talking to Mary and Joseph, who kneel before him. Above all three adult figures stands Anna with arms stretched out in vigorous amazement. In fact, the whole scene is one of contrast. There is a sense of the casual about the position of Jesus, on whom light shines from the upper left. There is an intensity about the way in which Simeon is speaking to Mary, whose eyes seem to stand out on stalks as they gaze across at her child. Joseph, who has his back to us, is nonetheless equally involved.

That painting expresses some of the contradictions with which today's festival has been laden. Whose feast is it? The 1662 Prayer Book subtitles it 'commonly called the Purification of St Mary the Virgin', borrowing from the late medieval custom. In the Eastern Orthodox Church, and throughout the Byzantine rite, it is called the 'Hypapante' – 'meeting'. Such an encounter includes everyone, but most importantly Christ. There are some traditions, moreover, which called this day 'St Simeon', falling into line with so many other occasions in the Christian calendar – one saint for one day!

Some of these contradictions go back to Luke's narrative itself, for it is – once more – a very *Lucan* festival, based exclusively on one Gospel writer's narrative (Luke 2:22–40). In the Temple drama Luke himself conflates the 'purification' of Mary after childbirth (something necessary for every mother, hence the two turtle doves or pigeons), and the 'presentation' (more accurately, the redemption) of the firstborn son. To compound the anomaly, Luke speaks of 'their' purification almost as if it were a kind of family liturgy. Why?

One answer would be to suggest that Luke is writing for a Gentile non-Palestinian community to whom the niceties of Jewish Temple ritual mattered little. The alternative is to suggest that Luke got it all wrong and did not know what he was writing about. But whatever the answer, subtleties are everywhere present. In contrast to John the Baptist, who has only Zechariah his father to proclaim his birth, Jesus has angels and then Simeon. The angels proclaim Christ as the expectation of Israel (Luke 2:10–11), whereas Simeon speaks of Christ fulfilling his destiny, 'in the presence of all peoples' (Luke 2:31). The balanced picture of devout parents with their child is enhanced by two aged people, who typify the Jewish-Christian devout poor, totally dependent upon God, seeing in Christ their deliverance.

Contrasts continue. Simeon is looking for the 'consolation' (Luke 2:25) of Israel, whereas Anna, the prophetess, speaks of the 'redemption' (Luke 2:38) which Christ will bring. Both Simeon's oracles, the Nunc Dimittis (Luke 2:29–32) and the warning to Mary about a sword piercing her own soul (Luke 2:34–5) rely on Isaiah's prophecy about consolation to Israel (e.g. Isa. 40:1ff.) As to the oracles themselves, the first sings of the reflections of the aged pious one, Simeon. It is a theme that persists in Christian spirituality, right down to the tenor and bass solos in liturgical settings of the canticle, and is particularly poignant in J. S. Bach's Cantata for this day, '*Ich habe genug*' (It is enough).

The Nunc Dimittis is so embedded in the Offices of Evening Prayer and Compline in the West that it is hard for us to realize that in the medieval West, it was used primarily on this day during the distribution of candles before the Eucharist, and only gradually came to be used in the last of the daily prayers of the Church. It could be that the Nunc Dimittis does not belong to the original version of this part of Luke's Gospel either. The second oracle, however, the prophecy that a sword shall pierce Mary's own soul also, raises serious issues. Rather than trying to iron out harshnesses, it is better to accept them. Mary is the first to hear of the good news of Jesus and is also the first to encounter its challenge, and the tragedy of its rejection by many in Israel. Luke's portrait of Christ, ambivalent about family loyalties, is perhaps saying that being related to Jesus is not enough. The passage ends with the statement that Jesus 'grew and became strong, filled with wisdom: and the favour of God was upon him' (Luke 2:40). John the Baptist, on the other hand, was 'strong in Spirit', but Jesus already has the Spirit.

What, then, of the gospel story? It would appear that the drama is too complex for one theme to dominate. Luke's narrative is both of purification and presentation, it is both a meeting with Simeon and Anna, and an encounter between the believer and the Christ. Similarly, Luke's Christ is always both divine and a human and trusting figure, ready to identify with the forgotten elements of society (here, an old man and a woman too), and this must arouse conflict from the start. Whereas Matthew's sign of early tragedy is the slaying of the innocents (see 28 December), Luke's is the deliberate juxtaposition of the oracle of departure (Nunc Dimittis) and the oracle of tragic future. The narrative, then, already contains the seeds for careful and varied treatment in the liturgy.

But what of Anna? Iconography comes to our help. Sometimes in the West, both Simeon and Anna appear – as in the Rembrandt painting. But in the East, Anna is always there. This is reflected by the length of the gospel passage for today. In the East, it invariably continues to verse 40, whereas in the West it usually ends at verse 32, after the Nunc Dimittis. In the first Prayer Books (1549 and 1552), this latter tradition was followed, but in 1662 (perhaps because John Cosin knew of the Eastern tradition!) Anna is at last included and the gospel passage ends at verse 40. In our own day, it is of vital importance that both Simeon and Anna are included in the celebration, particularly as the place of women is an honoured one in Luke's Gospel – as it should be in our Church today.

The festival is first come across in the diary of a nun called Egeria from France or Spain, who visited Jerusalem probably between 381 and 384. She describes a special celebration of the Eucharist at which the *whole* passage was obviously read. The liturgical use of candles, suggested by the Nunc Dimittis (a light to lighten the Gentiles, Luke 2:32), we first encounter a century afterwards; it may also have been a physical convenience in a pre-dawn Eucharist in early spring. In the West, Pope Sergius I (687–701), who came from a Syrian family and therefore knew about Eastern customs, introduced a procession before the Eucharist on this day, as well as on the Annunciation (25 March), the Assumption and the Nativity of the Virgin Mary (15 August and 8 September). Such an imaginative use of liturgy in the open spaces of urban life then was a feature of what we know to have been popular at the time in Jerusalem, Constantinople and Rome.

When people came to church to receive something, whether candles on 2 February, ash on Ash Wednesday, or palm crosses on Palm Sunday, there was an understandable trend to bless them. From the ninth century onwards, prayers for blessing the candles on this day begin to appear in the Sacramentaries, sometimes added and probably the result of 'ad-lib' composition, as on some occasions today. Some of the texts produced are fascinating, including one which refers to wax as 'the liquor of bees'. Others, moreover, speak of the light of Christ shining as a result of Christ's Presentation in the Temple. As formalization took over, the blessing became more complex, and the distribution as well. It is no surprise that the title 'Candlemas' survived the Reformation in popular usage both in Lutheran Germany and in the Church of England. *The Promise of His Glory* (1991) builds on this tradition by providing for a procession, and the distribution of candles. Moreover, it tries to draw out the 'bitter-sweet' character of this festival, with its joy as well as its prophecy of future suffering, and even suggests that this feast is a 'hinge' between Christmas and Lent.

Today's feast is indeed a rich one. Even though it is based on a narrative from only one of the Gospels, it provides a great deal of spiritual sustenance, which is why one can return to it year by year and see something new. The Collect for today is adapted from the Prayer Book, which in turn comes from the Gregorian Sacramentary: Christ was presented to God today in the Temple, and so we pray that we may be presented 'with pure and clean hearts'. The Old Testament reading, slightly expanded from the medieval lection for the epistle, prophesies that the messenger will prepare the way of the Lord and 'will suddenly come to his Temple' (Mal. 3:1–5). The epistle itself, the result of recent revisions, affirms that Christ is not concerned with angels but 'with the descendants of Abraham' (Heb. 2:14–18): Christ comes to the centre of the worship for the descendants of Abraham, and is made known there. The gospel tells this marvellous story, in all its richness (Luke 2:22–40). And the Post-Communion Prayer, adapted from the new Roman rite, draws both Simeon and Anna into the welcome of the Messiah, and suggests the Eastern title of this feast as we 'prepare to meet Christ Jesus when he comes to bring us to eternal life'.

Whether we actually use candles or not, the bearing of light is a strong suggestion from the gospel. One of the great preachers of the seventeenth century was Mark Frank (c.1612–64). Here is a short extract from one of his sermons on this day:

> Take them, and take him; the candle of faith will there show you him, and the candle of charity will light him down into your arms, that you may embrace him. We embrace where we love, we take into our arms whom we love; so that love Jesus and embrace Jesus – love Jesus and take Jesus – love Jesus and take him into our hands, and into our arms, and into our mouths, and into our hearts.

Fifty-One Sermons by Dr Mark Frank, Library of Anglo-Catholic Theology (Oxford: Parker, 1849), p. 358.

Joseph of Nazareth

19 March (Festival – White)

If there is one figure in the Nativity scene who could be said to
suffer from neglect, it is Joseph of Nazareth. This is partly
because the New Testament tells us very little about him. Apart
from the infancy narratives at the beginning of Matthew and
Luke there is virtually no mention of him, except the question
'Is not this Joseph's son?' (Luke 4:22) or the more oblique form
of that question, 'Is not this the carpenter's son?' (Matt. 13:55).
But art and religious legend take over. He is often depicted as
much older than Mary, as in the medieval carol, 'Joseph was
an old man'. And in some paintings, he is depicted with grey
hairs, groping around for five shekels (Num. 3:47) in order to
pay for the poor man's offering in the Temple at the Presentation
of Christ (2 February). He is even often referred to as chaste,
hence the tradition of him holding a lily.

But he still gets a mixed press! The *History of Joseph the
Carpenter* written in Greek in several forms in the fifth and sixth
centuries, and which spread from there to the West, contains
the seeds of many of the legends associated with him. Many
churches, hospitals and religious congregations are dedicated to
him in the later Middle Ages, perhaps to counteract the Mystery
Plays which reflected a popular tendency to make him appear
a fool and not a serious part of the story at all. Some traditions
latch on to his trade as a carpenter, and emphasize his poverty.
The economic standing of such a trade can be variously interpreted. Some nowadays would have us believe that Jesus was
brought up in a very comfortable existence, which might explain
the journey which Luke describes from Nazareth to Bethlehem

for the census (Luke 2:1–7). But the intention of the Gospel writers seems clearly to indicate an obscure and modest background for Jesus of Nazareth.

Unlike the other principal New Testament saints, Joseph took some time to get into the calendar at all. In Egypt in the fifth century he was already celebrated on 20 March, and he does appear in some early calendars, from the tenth century onwards, in the West. But it is not until the fourteenth and fifteenth centuries, and under Franciscan influence (as with the Feast of the Holy Name), that his commemoration on this day begins to find strong ground. He does not appear in the Prayer Book and he was universally imposed on the Roman Catholic Church only after the Reformation.

The portrait of Joseph is confined to the infancy narratives of Matthew and Luke. These are essentially different in their focus. Whereas in Luke, Mary is the prominent figure, and it is to her that Gabriel speaks directly (Luke 1:26–38) at the Annunciation (see 25 March), Joseph is the more prominent figure in Matthew's Gospel; the angel of the Lord appears to him in a dream telling him not to put aside Mary, pregnant by the Holy Spirit (Matt. 1:18–25); and it is Joseph, again at the spurring of an angel appearing to him in a dream, that takes the initiative to travel to and from Egypt in order to avoid Herod (Matt. 2:13–15, 19–23).

Today's festival can therefore justifiably be described as *Matthean*, and appropriately so, in view of the Annunciation which follows in six days' time, which is essentially *Lucan* (25 March). Indeed, Matthew's Gospel begins by stressing Jesus' Davidic descent: 'The Book of the Genealogy of Jesus Christ, The Son of David, The Son of Abraham' (Matt. 1:1); and David appears at the end of that list, so 'all the generations from Abraham to David were fourteen generations, and from David to the deportation to Babylon fourteen generations, and from the deportation to Babylon to Christ fourteen generations' (Matt. 1:17). The male descent of Joseph locates him firmly in the historic tradition of Judaism, which is very much Matthew's priority as the most Jewish of the Gospel writers. For even though Jesus is the Son of God, he is still also the Son of Joseph. He is a devout and faithful son of Judaism, whose birth and life and death are to transform that faith into the fuller purposes of the God of Israel.

All four Gospels concentrate on Jesus fulfilling, in one way or another, the Old Testament. This is especially the case in Matthew's Gospel. Jesus' Davidic descent comes across all the more powerfully in this Gospel since the birth takes place at Bethlehem, without any mention of a journey from Nazareth at all. Joseph as the earthly father of Jesus is in charge. He is directed on his way by a combination of two traditional means of divine inspiration, angels and dreams. The flight into Egypt emphasizes further the insecure world into which Jesus was born. Egypt was a favourite place of asylum for unwanted Jews, and Matthew is suggesting that Jesus spent his very early life among one or other of the Jewish communities there. But Egypt to any early Jewish-Christian audience will also have suggested Israel's supreme formative experience – the Exodus. This new saviour had to experience life there in order to bring about the greater liberation which his death and resurrection was to inaugurate. Indeed, one of the features in Matthew's Gospel is this *presence* of Christ in the world. The words of the prophet that the Virgin's son should be called Emmanuel (Matt. 1:23, cf. Isa. 7:14) begin the Gospel, and this divine presence is repeated at the end when he says, 'And lo, I am with you always, to the close of the age' (Matt. 28:20). Joseph's role, therefore, is to be around when he is needed, namely at the birth of Christ. And he disappears thereafter, his task done.

Today's celebration was introduced into *The Alternative Service Book (1980)* and other modern Anglican revisions. The Collect is a lightly revised version of the 1980 text, with the theme of 'Joseph the Worker'. The Old Testament reading, also in the other modern revisions, consists of the first part of Nathan's prophecy to David, that after David's death the succession will continue from son to son, and that a temple will be built to replace the temporary dwelling place of God in a tent (2 Sam. 7:4–16). Here is a rich echo of the incarnation. The epistle reading, on the other hand, also in the modern revisions, brings the promise to Abraham and his descendants into the life of faith today (Rom. 4:13–18). The gospel reading in *The Book of Common Prayer* (1979) of the Episcopal Church tells the tale of Mary and Joseph taking the twelve-year-old Jesus to Jerusalem when he is lost in the Temple (Luke 2:41– 52) – an often neglected part of the infancy narrative sequence. But the more generally used gospel for today is the narrative of the birth of Christ in Matthew, where Mary and Joseph are betrothed, Mary is already expecting a child, Joseph is warned in a dream not to put away the marriage contract – which in those days, he would have been entitled to do in the circum- stances, even though it was legally binding – and the birth itself (Matt. 1:18–25). The Post-Communion Prayer (perhaps over- subtly) works on the carpenter image, contrasting 'the wood of the cross' with the 'wisdom of the world as foolishness', echoing Paul's teaching to this effect at the beginning of his letter to the Corinthians (1 Cor. 1).

Joseph remains a mysterious figure. As we have suggested, Matthew deliberately brings him on to the stage when he is required, and he departs when his task is over. But as a devout and obedient father, his main hidden task was to bring up the child Jesus in a life of faithfulness and obedience. This is where the hidden days in Egypt and then later in Galilee must have been formative. F. W. Farrar (1831–1903), the famous Canon of Westminster (and grandfather of Field-Marshal Mont- gomery), wrote a book called *The Life of Christ* which was popular at the end of the last century. Of these hidden years, he writes as follows:

What was his manner of life during those thirty years? It is a question which the Christian cannot help asking in deep reverence and with yearning love; but the words in which the gospels answer it are very calm and very few ... there is, then, for the most part a deep silence in the evangelists respecting this period; but what eloquence in their silence! May we not find in their very reticence a wisdom and an instruction more profound than if they had filled many volumes with minor details?

F. W. Farrar, *The Life of Christ* (London: Cassell, 1884), pp. 24f.

The Annunciation of Our Lord to the Blessed Virgin Mary

25 March (Principal Feast – White or Gold)

Special occasions are almost doomed to get in the way – and that is their job. For to celebrate the Annunciation on 25 March does indeed place the conception of Jesus exactly nine months from his birth on 25 December, but the latter part of March inevitably falls either during the latter part of Lent or (exceptionally) immediately after Easter. For some people, this is an untidy and messy arrangement, and there were some calendars – notably in Spain in the early Middle Ages – which celebrated this occasion on 18 December, just before Christmas.

But there is method in the madness of the Christian calendar. For the birth and the death of Jesus are intrinsically linked. He was born to die, and he died because he was born in order to fulfil God's purposes. Indeed, birth and death are linked in the human process of reproduction in any case. And the matter is clinched when we consider the possibility that Christmas itself may have been calculated nine months away from a possible date for the death of Christ, as some early Christians understood it. Birth and death, creation and new creation, incarnation and atonement – call it what you will – in the Christian life, everything is connected to everything else. In any case, there are times when this feast can be a welcome break from Lenten solemnity.

The Annunciation is therefore a significant key to the nature and character of the Christian calendar. That may explain why – even allowing for its colourful drama – it is one of the most frequent scenes depicted in Christian art. The angel Gabriel appears to Mary and the facial and body language can be very subtle. Gabriel's strength of purpose and Mary's modesty of character have been exploited many times. Joseph sometimes appears off-stage in an adjacent scene setting mouse traps – a suggestion that the child that is to be born will forgive the sins of the world! But like the Presentation of Christ in the Temple (2 February), today's feast is linked to one episode in one Gospel: it is from Mary's perspective (not Joseph's) and is therefore essentially Lucan (Luke 1:26–38). This is always the reading for today.

The gospel passage repays careful attention. It begins by locating the scene to time and place – the sixth month, in Nazareth. Mary is already betrothed to Joseph, and the two characters in the scene are Gabriel and Mary. There are three exchanges between them. Gabriel greets her as highly favoured and Mary is too troubled to respond – a sign of her modesty. Gabriel tells her not to be afraid because she will conceive and bear a son who will be called Jesus. Mary replies straight away with a question – How? – an indication this time of the spirit of faithful enquiry. Gabriel replies by saying that the Holy Spirit will come upon her, and suggests that she is not to be too surprised, because her cousin Elizabeth in old age is already expecting a child, in accordance with the will of God. Mary responds with a statement that 'I am the handmaid of the Lord' – an indication this time of faithful trust. Both Mary and Zechariah before her responded with enquiry. Although slightly unfair on Zechariah Luke wants us to understand that Mary's enquiry is faithful and Zechariah's is unbelieving.

Mary's qualities are therefore apparent. When she is troubled she says nothing, because of her modesty. When she is told what is to happen in the future, she asks, 'How?' in faithful enquiry. When she knows the 'what' and the 'how', she commits herself to the Lord, in faithful trust. It is no wonder, therefore, that Christians of all traditions have in different ways looked to Mary as an example of faith – a faith that is prepared to be *reticent*, a faith that is ready to *enquire*, and a faith that is ready to *trust*. Christians find it easy to be immodest when troubled, too glibly unquestioning when persistent enquiry is the order of the day, and insufficiently trusting when the purposes of God begin slowly to break through. Not all may agree that we can look to her for her prayers in heaven, but we can certainly see in her a model for Christian discipleship.

Because of the powerful drama of this important episode in Luke's infancy narrative, the Annunciation scene was almost bound to become a principal feast in the calendar sooner or later. Abraham of Ephesus preached a sermon on it at Constantinople or Ephesus, between the years 530 and 553. It was already celebrated on this day in the mid-seventh century at Rome, and Pope Sergius I (687–701) added a procession before the Eucharist, as we have already seen in the case of the Presentation of Christ in the Temple (see 2 February). In the Eastern Orthodox tradition, and throughout the Byzantine rite, it became the practice to abstain from celebrating the Eucharist on ordinary weekdays in Lent. That this day was exempted indicates its importance. In the Middle Ages, it was referred to as the Annunciation of *Our Lady*, and as with Candlemas, one could argue the case either way: is it a feast of the Virgin Mary or of Our Lord? Modern revisions tend to opt for the latter, because it must ultimately point to the incarnation, and therefore to Christ himself. This is reflected in the Communion verse which has been sung for centuries in the Greek Orthodox Church today: 'The Lord has chosen Zion: he has desired her for his habitation' (Psalm 132:14).

The Collect for today goes back through the Prayer Book to the Gregorian Sacramentary. The Old Testament reading (in the Middle Ages the reading for the epistle) is the prophecy that the Virgin shall conceive (Isa. 7:10–14a). The epistle itself, which appears in the new revisions, sets the work of Christ above all sacrifices, for 'we have been sanctified through the offering of the body of Jesus Christ once for all' (Heb. 10:4–10). The Post-Communion Prayer is a fine meditation on the gospel passage; 'you visit us with your Holy Spirit and overshadow us by your power' in the eucharistic celebration; 'strengthen us to walk with Mary the joyful path of obedience and so to bring forth the fruits of holiness'.

*　　*　　*

Another of the great preachers of the seventeenth century was Herbert Thorndike (1598–1672), who became a Canon of Westminster after a distinguished career as a scholar. In the following passage he draws together many of the strands represented by today's feast:

> When therefore the angel Gabriel appeared to the blessed Virgin saying 'the Holy Ghost shall come upon thee and the most high shall overshadow thee, and therefore the Holy Thing that is born ... shall be called the son of God', we are to understand, that the Holy Ghost upon this message possessing the flesh of the blessed Virgin made it a tabernacle for the Word of God always to dwell in; in which Word the Spirit of God always dwelt. For so the difference holds between our Lord Christ in whom dwells the fullness of the Spirit and his servants which has each of them his measure of it; if we understand the Word Incarnate to have in it resident the presence of God's Spirit, by which our Lord Christ proved himself the Son of God.

The Theological Works of Herbert Thorndike, Library of Anglo-Catholic Theology (Oxford: Parker, 1849,) p. 248.

George, Martyr, Patron of England

23 April (Festival – Red)

Stockholm Cathedral is a large and impressive work of medieval gothic architecture. Built in the style of what are often referred to as the 'Hall Churches', it is spacious inside, and because nave, chancel and aisle are all of the same height, the visitor has a good view of everything from the moment of entry.

To the north of the high altar stands an enormous statue of George on his stallion about to slay the dragon, and nearby is another statue of the princess whom he saves, devoutly kneeling in prayer at her castle. The Nordic region had its fair share of internecine wars and the statue group is regarded as something of a national monument. The burghers of Stockholm were fortunate in the sculptor, Bernt Notke from Lubeck, who by 1489 had a renown that spread throughout the Nordic and Baltic worlds.

Dragon and horse are terrifyingly of similar size. As in other depictions of this subject, the dragon holds in his right front claw part of George's spear, which he had presumably broken in a previous attempt to slay him. But the charger stands over the already wounded beast and George has his sword gripped in both hands, ready to strike the fatal blow.

The scene is legendary, it has evoked violence and instability and the sad place of warfare in the development of our civilization. The George of history does not seem to have slain a dragon at all, for the legend that grew up around him in the Middle Ages owes more to the ancient Greek myth of Theseus slaying the Minotaur! He may well have been a soldier, but the fact that he was martyred in Palestine before Christianity

emerged from its persecution ensured him a place in the collec-
tive memory of the Christian Church. Like so many local martyrs, he became a figure of inspiration, a link between the
apostolic Church of the first century, in all those wondrous New
Testament figures, and the Church of 'my own time' and 'my
own place'.

The Greeks named him the 'great martyr'. We come across
him in the West in the Gregorian Sacramentary, the book of
prayers for the sacraments that reflects the practice of the Roman
Church from the seventh century onwards. He was seen very
much as a local saint, which explains why churches were dedicated to him in Jerusalem and Antioch, and he was often invoked
as a patron saint of the armies of the Byzantine Empire.

George was known in England from around the same time.
But it was after the Crusades that his cult grew in popularity in
England. Richard the Lionheart placed himself and his army
under George's protection. His feast was made a holy day at
the Synod of Oxford (1222), and in the following century
Edward III founded the Order of the Garter under his patronage
– hence the Chapel of St George at Windsor. He was fast becoming the Patron Saint of England. He was one of those saints who
survived into the calendars of the first Prayer Books, although no
specific liturgical provision was made for his day.

His day now ranks as a festival in the new calendar of the
Church of England, and uniquely so, since his place is due
entirely to his being the national patron saint. Many churches
have been dedicated to him across the centuries, and many of
our churches gather uniformed organizations, through the Scout
and Guide movements, around his date.

The Collect for today, written by Michael Perham (1947-),
who was Rector of a church dedicated to St George, spiritualizes
the legends associated with St George. God 'kindled the flame
of love in the heart of your servant George that he bore witness
to the risen Lord by his life and by his death'; and it goes on
to pray that 'we who rejoice in his triumphs may come to share
with him the fullness of the resurrection'. For the Old Testament

reading, we have a choice between Mattathias exhorting his sons to put their trust in God, and to be courageous (1 Macc. 2:59–64) or the vision of war in heaven, in which Michael and his angels fight the dragon (Rev. 12:7–12). The epistle likens the Christian life to the soldier on service, the athlete winning the prize, and the wise farmer (2 Tim. 2:3–13). The gospel, appropriate for a soldier martyr, is Christ's warning about persecution (John 15:18–21). For the Post-Communion Prayer, there is a choice between one based on the Roman provision for this day and a new composition. Both give thanks for the martyrdom of George, and pray that through the Eucharist we may be strengthened to witness to Christ's salvation.

George inevitably brings us through his legends face to face with the violence of warfare, and many who have looked to him in the past as their patron have also shuddered at the sheer scale of human suffering that warfare has brought. One of the most tragic conflicts of recent centuries was the Great War that was fought in Europe between 1914 and 1918. Historians continue to re-examine the details and to find a reason for it all. Whatever these reasons were, and however we may judge the conduct of the war (another question altogether), the legacy of the events of those years remains as a judgement on our whole way of life. In his classic study of the Church's response to this war, Alan Wilkinson (1931-) brings us to the heart of the matter:

> The fact that the Great War still haunts the communal memory suggests that we still have not yet completed our work of remembrance. If we have not already discovered it through other means, the Great War confronts us with the fact that there are no easy human or Christian answers to life, with its extraordinary mixture of tragedy and comedy, brutality and compassion, rationality and irrationality. It is the greatness of Christianity at its best that it affords no easy answers, but rather points us to the heart of the darkness unflinchingly, enables misery to be transmuted into pain and,

by making the darkness tangible, turns the apparent absence of God into a presence, however paradoxical and elusive that presence has to be, God being God.

Alan Wilkinson, *The Church of England and the First World War* (London: SCM Press, 1996), p. 310.

Mark the Evangelist

25 April (Festival – Red)

There are many different ways of telling a story. Some begin gradually with the background. Others come straight to the point, almost in a rush. Whereas Matthew and Luke take care to tell all manner of details about the circumstances of the birth of Christ, Mark plunges straight in: 'The beginning of the Gospel of Jesus Christ, the Son of God' (Mark 1:1). We are led into the wilderness to see John the Baptist preaching and Christ's baptism. It is not just the structure of Mark's Gospel that is brief, it is also his style which is abrupt. His Greek is simple and direct. It has none of the polish of Luke, and certainly nothing of the extended ruminations of the Fourth Gospel.

There are, indeed, no infancy narratives. But as if to make up for this, Mark's account of the children being brought to Jesus has some significant differences from those in Matthew and Luke. It is altogether a more dramatic scene (Mark 10:13–16). Jesus is indignant; Jesus tells his followers to receive the Kingdom of Heaven like a child; and he takes the children in his arms and blesses them. He is thus committed to three important aspects of the Christian faith. There are situations where indignation can be righteous. To enter the Kingdom of Heaven we have to be ready to take on the attributes of children, which means balancing innocence with relentless questioning. And part of that 'receiving' involves the very physical gesture of being taken in Christ's arms and being blessed. No wonder Martin Luther and Thomas Cranmer chose *that* particular version of the scene for their baptismal liturgies in the Prayer Books!

Mark's portrait of Christ may be the least polished of all the

Gospels from a stylistic point of view. But it is perhaps all the more powerful for that. Jesus is the Messiah, whose identity is disclosed slowly. The disciples are slow to understand. Peter's confession of Christ (Mark 8:27f.) suggests that even though at least one of his followers is able to express this identity, all of them continue to fail to grasp the full meaning. It is the same old story of the gap between verbal commitment and consistent discipleship – in which we all fail. Mark's passion narrative, moreover, tells of a man who goes to his death in utter loneliness: the disciples sleep in the garden, they desert him at his arrest, and Peter denies him (Mark 14:32–72). But the good news is for *all*, and the pagan centurion is the first to confess him to be the Son of God (Mark 15:39). Many scholars agree with early manuscripts that Mark's Gospel should end just after the Easter morning scene, when the disciples leave the tomb in trembling and astonishment, 'for they were afraid' (Mark 16:8). In all the celebrations so far in the calendar, the liturgical colour has been white or gold. It is appropriate that the first one for which red is directed should be this, the starkest of all the Gospel writers.

But which Mark is the author of this Gospel? Is he the young man who followed Christ with nothing on but a linen cloth (Mark 14:41)? Is he the cousin of Barnabas, the companion of Paul and Peter (Acts 13:15)? After falling out with Paul, he is reconciled to him (Col. 4:10, Phil. 1:23). Peter mentions him as 'his son' (1 Pet. 5:13). An early Christian writer called Papias described Mark as an 'interpreter' of Peter. There are persistent traditions associating Mark both with Alexandria and with Rome; and it may be that Peter was responsible for sending him from Rome to Alexandria. The Coptic Church celebrates a Liturgy ascribed to Mark (but clearly not written by him) on special occasions. On the other hand, scholars see in Mark's Gospel suggestions that it was written for Christians in Rome, which would explain the link with Peter. Just to complicate matters further, the relics of Mark were brought from Alexandria to Venice in 828/9, in order to keep them safe from Arab invasion. And St Mark's, Venice has some mosaics from the twelfth and thirteenth centuries giving a life of Mark.

It could be that all these details derive from a common source. Their relationship with each other continues to be disputed. But the fact remains that, from an early date, Mark has been celebrated on this day in all the Eastern Churches (Copts, Syrians, Byzantines), which suggests that they had been doing so from before the time of their divisions from each other, in the fourth century. But although there was a church dedicated to St Mark in Rome in the early fourth century, he does not enter the Western calendars until the late eighth, along with a number of other New Testament figures, such as Philip and James, James the Great, Bartholomew, and Matthew.

In iconography, Mark is usually represented by a lion. This figure is derived from the four living creatures round the throne in heaven (Rev. 4:2–8; cf. Ezek. 1:10). Christian writers have been conscious of the different characteristics of each one of the evangelists long before the biblical criticism of recent centuries! Indeed in the early centuries, Christian writers identified the four evangelists with these four creatures. The lion suggests strength; John, as the most prophetic of the Gospel writers, is symbolized by the eagle; Luke, with his sensitivity to Christ's patience and innocence, is symbolized by the ox; and Matthew, with his portrayal of Christ the teacher focused on the Sermon on the Mount, is symbolized by the man. It is a somewhat arbitrary series of identifications, but nonetheless a persistent one in iconography, Eastern as well as Western.

Today's Collect is adapted from the Prayer Book with its indication of Mark's strength, 'being firmly grounded in the truth of the gospel'. The Old Testament reading provides teaching for the development of wisdom, in line with Mark's portrayal of Christ spreading his teaching throughout the Gospel (Prov. 15:18–23). The alternative reading from Acts tells of the disagreement between John, Mark and Paul (Acts 15:35–41), a comfort for many a faithful Christian. The epistle tells us of the gifts of the ascended Christ in their different forms of ministry (Eph. 4:7–16). And the gospel is addressed to the disciples on the Mount of Olives about what the future would hold, and the nature and cost of discipleship (Mark 13:5–13). The Post-Communion Prayer provision we have seen before, either the second collect from *The Alternative Service Book (1980)* or a prayer from the Canadian *Book of Alternative Services* (1985).

Each Gospel writer repays study and meditation. Each one has his own character. In his Hulsean sermon at Great St Mary's, Cambridge, Austin Farrer (1906–68) had these prophetic words to say:

> The only Mark we want is the Mark who became, for an unknown number of days and hours, the inspired act of meditating and writing this book. We want nothing but his mental life, and of his mental life no more than is enclosed between the first verse of his first chapter and the eighth of his sixteenth. If this is a whole, living, personal and continuous mental act, and I can touch it, then I can touch the vital and significant part of that web of life which made up the substance of Christian origins; and from it my thought can spread to other unconnected parts of the web, and ultimately the centre, which is Christ himself.
>
> Austin Farrer, *A Celebration of Faith* (London: Hodder & Stoughton, 1970), p. 41.

Philip and James, Apostles

1 May (Festival – Red)

In one of his sermons, Gregory the Great remarked that Our Lord sent his disciples out two by two, showing that no-one should be given the task of preaching the gospel if he did not love his brother. In Philip and James – like Simon and Jude (28 October) – we come across a pair of apostles who have been thrown together, not by Jesus, but by the accidents of the Christian calendar. No doubt the strategy for mission that we see in the Gospels (e.g. Luke 10:1) suggested such pairing. But Philip and James are linked in the West only because of the curious fact that *c.*570 the dedication took place of a basilica in Rome of the 'Holy Apostles' in which their relics were deposited. (In the East, Philip is celebrated on 14 November, and James on 9 October.)

Both of them appear in the lists of the Apostles (Matt. 10:3; Mark 3:18; Luke 6:14; Acts 1:13). These lists were important for the authentication of the early leadership of the Church as it spread from locality to locality and needed a sense of catholicity. Clearly names of particular apostles were associated with particular places, and 'The Twelve' together with others after them were foundational figures. A name is not a statistic, but a person; and in Christian terms, a person called by God, through Christ, in the power of the Spirit, to fulfil the missionary imperative of the Church.

When one looks at the Gospels, however, Philip and James appear to be somewhat unequally matched. The James in question is 'son of Alphaeus', often called James the Less, in order to distinguish him from James the Great (25 July). But just because James has no significant role in the Gospels other than appearing among the lists of the original twelve, that does not mean to say that he was of no importance. Christ continues to call people today, whether or not they hit the headlines as martyrs or teachers or holy men and women, for all people who follow Christ in any way become holy men and holy women.

Philip, on the other hand, appears on a number of occasions, and exclusively in the Fourth Gospel. It is for that reason that he can be called a Johannine figure. First of all, Philip appears in Bethsaida, Galilee, and is called by Andrew to meet Christ. Philip then finds Nathanael (is this possibly Bartholomew? – 24 August), who is somewhat sceptical at first about Jesus. Philip, therefore, is on the scene early in the calling of the disciples and he has the enthusiasm to face those reluctant to come forward (John 1:43–8).

Secondly, Philip makes an appearance in the wilderness when Jesus is confronted with 5,000 hungry people. It is to Philip that Jesus asks the question, 'How are we to buy bread?', and Philip replies that 200 denarii would not be enough (John 6:5,7). That little exchange is significant, because Jesus is testing him out. It is as if Philip knows that something extraordinary is going to happen but is not quite sure.

Thirdly, when Jesus has entered Jerusalem for his final Passover, some Greeks appear, presumably also in order to celebrate the Jewish Passover in Jerusalem, and they want to see Jesus. It is to Philip that they express their request (John 12:21,22). Philip is an accessible figure for those who could easily feel outside the Christian faith, and there have even been suggestions that his Greek name ('Philip' means 'lover of horses'!) made him something of a go-between.

And fourthly, after the Last Supper, when Jesus has washed the feet of the disciples, it is Philip who asks the question – almost with exasperation – 'Lord, show us the Father, and we shall be satisfied' (John 14:8). Philip seems to be aware that the drama of Christ's life is reaching a climax, and he wants all revealed. But he has yet to realize that it is *Jesus* who is already the manifestation of God for the human race.

Philip and James are both supposed to have been martyred. Philip is said to have been crucified head down, but there is a legend in *The Apocryphal Acts of Philip* (an early collection of tales about him) which depicts him killing a fire-breathing dragon. He is supposed to have preached in Phrygia, and the place of his martyrdom is sometimes identified with Hierapolis. He is often painted with loaves of bread – echoing his important role before the feeding of the five thousand. James, on the other hand, is supposed to have been condemned to death by the Sanhedrin in AD 62 and beaten to death by clubs. Philip and James are often depicted together in Western medieval art, because of their appearance together in the calendar, in the late eighth century. In the Roman Catholic calendar they were moved to 3 May in 1969 in order to make way for 'Joseph the Worker' on 1 May. But modern Anglican calendars retain the ancient date.

Today's Collect is derived from that of the Prayer Book, which echoes the words of Christ in the gospel passage – 'The Way, the Truth and the Life'. The Old Testament reading exhorts us to be reflective in our enthusiasm ('in returning and rest you shall be saved; in quietness and trust shall be your strength'), and goes on to prophesy that 'your teacher will not hide himself anymore, but your eyes shall see your teacher' (Isa. 30:15–21). This looks forward to what has been the traditional gospel passage for today, probably one of the central passages of the 'farewell discourses' in the Fourth Gospel (John 14:1–14). The epistle, suitably enough, is the opening hymn in Ephesians on the work of God, who has 'made known to us in all wisdom and insight the mystery of his will, according to his purpose which he set forth in Christ' (Eph. 1:3–10). The Post-Communion Prayer provision we have seen before, either the second Pentecost collect from *The Alternative Service Book (1980)* or a prayer from the Canadian *Book of Alternative Services* (1985).

The 'farewell discourses' of John's Gospel have been studied and meditated upon constantly. H. B. Swete (1835–1917), in an extended series of reflections, has this to say about Philip, about whom we know, understandably, more than his running mate of today:

> Of Philip as of Thomas our knowledge comes chiefly from St John. He was of Bethsaida, the fishing town on the sea which also gave to the Apostolate St Andrew and St Peter. The Lord had found and called Philip after his return to Galilee from the baptism. It was Philip who had answered Nathaniel's doubt; whom the Lord had proved by the question, 'where are we to buy bread that these may eat?'; to whom the Greeks, perhaps attracted by his Greek name, came with a petition, 'Sir, we would see Jesus'; and who, with Andrew, 'told Jesus' of their desire. And now it is Philip who, when he hears that he and his fellow disciples henceforth know the Father, and have even seen him, cannot repress the cry, 'Lord, show us the Father, and we shall ask nothing more.' . . . All those months in Galilee they had seen the God of Israel in the face of Jesus Christ; they had lived with the Father's very image, and had not known it.

H. B. Swete, *The Last Discourse and Prayer of Our Lord* (London: Macmillan, 1913), pp. 21f.

Matthias the Apostle

14 May (Festival – Red)

We know just a little bit more about Matthias than about James the Less. But unlike James, Matthias' role in the sequence of events is more important than what he is supposed to have achieved. And whereas Philip is a Johannine figure, Matthias is Lucan – not from the Gospel, but from the Acts of the Apostles. Indeed, it is the narrative from that work which supplies the foundation for today's celebration (Acts 1:15–26).

Who was to replace Judas Iscariot? Whatever the exact truth behind the need for an inner core of 'The Twelve', whether during Christ's life or in the early mission of the Church after the ascension, the fact remains that Luke found it necessary early on in his second book, which narrates that mission, to tell how one of the first things that the disciples did after the ascension was to gather and choose – under Peter's leadership – someone to replace him. Peter gives the criterion: 'So one of the men who have accompanied us during all the time that the Lord Jesus went in and out among us, beginning from the baptism of John until the day when he was taken up from us – one of these men must become one with us, a witness to his resurrection' (Acts 1:21f.). Here we have another commemoration, this time one intimately associated with one particular event, supplying the foundation for a significant day in the Christian calendar.

There are others who had followed Christ from the beginning but who had not been mentioned. According to Luke, in order to qualify as an apostle one had to have been a follower of Christ from his baptism to his ascension. The liturgical implications are clear. To be a witness to resurrection means witnessing Christ's

baptism and ascension. We have already seen the way in which
Luke has influenced important events in the formation of the
Christian calendar, as witness the Presentation in the Temple (2
February) and the Annunciation (25 March). There is yet more
to come, for example the Visit of the Virgin Mary to Elizabeth
(31 May), and the Ascension itself, to name but two. It is inevitable that Luke's historical scope should provide that kind of
liturgical sustenance.

Matthias is commemorated on different dates. The Copts have
4 May, the Syrians and Byzantines 9 August, and in the West
he has been kept on 24 February – and remains so in *The Book
of Common Prayer* (1979). After the Second Vatican Council,
the Roman Catholic Church moved him to 14 May, in order to
be near the Ascension and Pentecost, which is where he is to be
found in the Church of England revised calendar as well. As to
the date of his entry into the calendar, he is one of the saints, like
Barnabas and Luke, who does not appear until the ninth-century
Sacramentaries. Because of his obscurity, traditions vary about
him. Many preachers such as Eusebius and Epiphanius identify
him among the seventy disciples sent out by Christ (Luke
10:1ff.). There are traditions that he preached in Ethiopia, in
Cappadocia, and near the Caspian Sea. He is presumed to have
been martyred, and his relics are supposed to have been taken
to Trier, at St Matthias' Abbey. But whatever the truth of his
eventual whereabouts, his ultimate significance lies in his calling
to replace Judas and to make up the number of The Twelve to
completion.

The Collect for today is a modern version of that contained
in the Prayer Book, and the Post-Communion Prayers are once
again taken from Pentecost in *The Alternative Service Book
(1980)*, and from the Canadian *Book of Alternative Services*
(1985). The Old Testament reading is Isaiah's prophecy that
Shebna, the steward, will be cast down and replaced by Elikiam,
the son of Hilkiah (Isa. 22:15–25). The narrative of the choosing
of Matthias – by the traditional method of casting lots and by
prayer – is clearly obligatory today (Acts 1:15–26). If an epistle

reading is required, one is provided which exhorts stewards to be faithful (1 Cor. 4:1–7). In the medieval Roman scheme of readings, the gospel passage was Christ's prayer of thanksgiving that 'these things' have been hidden from the wise and learned and revealed to babes, and the challenge to come to him, as his burden is light (Matt. 11:25–30). However, there has been a tendency to choose the gospel from the 'farewell discourses'. The Prayer Book choice is the command to love one another (John 15:12–16), a slightly expanded version of which is generally used nowadays (John 15:9–17).

Matthias replaces Judas. In a sermon in St Paul's Cathedral, J. B. Lightfoot (1828–89), reflects on the fate of Judas and the faithfulness of the other apostles:

> Do not believe it, when they tell you that hope is a glamour, an illusion, a phantom light tempting you into a morass, alluring you to your destruction. Hope is the reflection of God's mercy; hope is the echo of God's love. Hope is energy, hope is strength, hope is life. Without hope sorrow for sin will lead only to ruin . . . We have no time to brood over the errors of the past, while the hours are hurrying relentlessly by; no time to tell our wounds and reckon up our slain, while the fight is still raging and the enemy is upon us. There is enough to occupy all our energies in this warfare of life, without wasting them on lost opportunities and profitless regrets.

> J. B. Lightfoot, *Sermons in St Paul's Cathedral* (London: Macmillan, 1891), p. 120.

The Visit of the Virgin Mary
to Elizabeth

31 May (Festival – White)

One of my favourite stained glass windows is in Chartres Cathedral. It consists of a series of panels recounting the life of the Virgin Mary. The two that always catch my eye depict the scenes commemorated on 25 March and today, namely the Annunciation and the Visit. On the left-hand side are to be seen the two figures of Gabriel and the Virgin Mary in their curious and surprising relationship. Then on the right-hand side are the two pregnant women. Mary is bouncing with joy and looks at her cousin Elizabeth, clad in duller clothes and looking older and more haggard. Even given the high-profile artistic context of a stained glass window in a medieval cathedral, the scene still cries out as being two expectant mothers meeting each other to discuss exactly what the future holds for them – and their offspring.

This is exactly the scene of today's commemoration. We are back, once more, to Luke's narrative. He it is who gives us the principal Marian feasts, and it is also he who gives us (as we shall see) a fuller account of John the Baptist than any of the other Gospel writers. It is, once again, a festival geared exclusively to one particular narrative (Luke 1:39–45). Here are the mother of Christ and the mother of John the Baptist meeting, prior to the birth of their children. Underneath the surface of this meeting, what does the Gospel tell us?

Mary seems to have made quite a journey from Galilee in the north to the hill country in Judea, something of a feat for a young girl who is pregnant. This must indicate determination on her part to seek support from her kinship and perhaps to

get away from families and friends in her immediate locality who
might be asking embarrassing questions. Suddenly everything
changes. Elizabeth's baby leaps in her womb, as the unborn
John the Baptist recognizes the mother of the Saviour who is to
come. From the beginning, therefore, John the Baptist is subordi-
nate to Jesus. Already John the Baptist is the Forerunner, as he
is invariably described in Eastern iconography. It is Christ to
whom he points. And he does so even before he is born! Then
Elizabeth becomes excited and utters beautiful words, which
come across somewhat incoherently. She acclaims Mary as
'blessed among women'. She expresses surprise that 'the mother
of my Lord' should come to her – already Jesus is Lord before
he is born. Then she states what has happened – that the babe
leapt the moment that Mary's greeting was heard. Excitement
indeed! Finally, she recognizes that Mary has had the faith to
believe what was told her by God, a reason for her to be called
'blessed'.

Here is Luke's characteristic desire to push as far back as he
possibly can the meaning of salvation in Christ in the ordinary
events in human life before Jesus himself was even conscious of
them. It is not enough for Jesus suddenly to appear in the wilderness as an adult – as in Mark's narrative. In order to hold on
to the *historic* character of Christ's Messiahship, of his being
Son of God, of his being the Saviour in deed as well as in name,
God has to be seen to be working before human awareness, not
only in the processes of initial human reproduction, but in events
and experiences surrounding pregnancy itself. If Luke was
indeed a physician, he would have known well just how sensitive
the bodies and minds and feelings of expectant mothers can be.

But when did this festival originate? Like the Holy Name and
St Joseph, it is of Franciscan origin in the West. Bonaventura,
the Superior-General of the Franciscans, decreed it for the use
of his Order in 1263. It was subsequently directed throughout
the West in 1389. But there is, nonetheless, evidence that it was
kept in Jerusalem as far back as the fifth century, if not earlier,
as a 'Feast of the Ark', corresponding with the arrival of the

Ark of the Covenant at the house of Abinadab (1 Sam. 7:1). Moreover, when David danced before the Lord when the Ark was finally brought to Jerusalem, the word used in the Greek version of the Old Testament is 'leap' (2 Sam. 6:14). Mary is sometimes seen as 'The Ark' of the New Testament, and this may explain such a celebration in Jerusalem, where from the fourth century onwards it became increasingly important to build churches or chapels and use the calendar in order to commemorate events narrated in the New Testament. The Western date, however, was 2 July, and this is where today's festival stands in the Prayer Book calendar, though – as with Mary Magdalene, the Transfiguration, and Holy Cross – there were no Collect or readings provided. But the opportunity was taken to move this festival back to today in the revision of the calendars following the example of the Roman Catholic Church after the Second Vatican Council, in order to provide some space around Petertide (29 June).

The Collect for today is a lightly enriched version of that which appears in *The Alternative Service Book (1980)*. The Old Testament reading suggests that 'Ark' image as the daughter of Zion must sing aloud (Zeph. 3:14–18). The epistle exhorts us not to flag in zeal, but to rejoice with those who rejoice and weep with those who weep (Rom. 12:9–16). Both these readings, though eminently appropriate, are the result of the recent revisions. The gospel passage permits either going right to the end of the Song of Mary (the Magnificat) or finishing a third of the way through (Luke 1:39–49, [50–56]). The Post-Communion Prayer, like that written for the Annunciation (25 March), reflects tenderly on the gospel passage as Elizabeth and Mary 'recognize the signs of redemption at work within them'.

The Magnificat is the real song for today. Mary has not only shown her modesty, her trustful enquiry, and her faithful obedience to the angel Gabriel (see the Annunciation on 25 March). Now she has witnessed the recognition of this promise in the way in which Elizabeth and her unborn son have responded to her. On the basis of these encounters, she can sing of the wonders of the Lord, of his faithfulness, his mercy, and his determination to break through into human history and reverse the contrasts that we humans have placed as obstacles before the coming of his Kingdom. The song ends, but the visit goes on – for three months. That would see Elizabeth through towards the end of her pregnancy, and Mary well into hers.

Something of these sentiments inspired Jeremy Taylor (1613–67) to write in the following way in his classic devotional Life of Christ, the very first of its kind, in 1649:

> When her cousin Elizabeth saw the mother of her Lord come to visit her, as the Lord himself descended to visit all the world in great humility, she was pleased and transported to the height of wonder and prophecy and 'the babe sprang in her womb', and was sanctified . . . But if Saint Elizabeth was carried into ecstasy, wondering at the dignation and favour done to her by the mother of her Lord; with what preparations and holy solemnities ought we to entertain his addresses to us by his Holy Sacrament, by the Immissions of his Spirit, by the assistances of his Graces, and all other vouchsafings and descents into our hearts?

> Jeremy Taylor, *The Great Exemplar*, Vol. II, Section II, Add. Sec. II.

Barnabas the Apostle

11 June (Festival – Red)

The name Barnabas has often been taken to mean 'Son of encouragement', or 'Son of consolation'. Something of those characteristics shines through from what we know of him in the pages of the New Testament. Once again, he is an essentially Lucan figure, although there are references to his close companionship with Paul in the Epistles (1 Cor. 9:6; Gal. 2:1,9, 13; Col. 4:10). He was one of the first disciples at Jerusalem (Acts 4:36) and having arrived with one name (Joseph) was surnamed Barnabas by the apostles themselves. This probably indicates that he won a special place in the mission of the Church at an early stage. He was a Levite from Cyprus and therefore is a typical figure in the background of Luke's narrative in the Acts of the Apostles, since he was a Jew living in the diaspora.

Luke tells us that he took part in Paul's first two missionary journeys, first of all to Cyprus, Barnabas' home territory, then to Antioch in Pisidia, and Lycaonia and Lystra, Derbe and to Antioch in Syria (Acts 13:1–14:28). The Council in Jerusalem in the next chapter (Acts 15:1–29) saw Barnabas backing up Paul in his insistence that Gentiles did not have to be circumcised before they became Christians. Paul then set out on his second missionary journey, but because he and Barnabas disagreed over John Mark's steadiness when they had been in Pamphylia together (Acts 13:13), they separated. The rift was probably more about which companions they should take than a major personal difference of opinion between them, for they remained friends later on. This should not be a surprise, given the fact that Barnabas had been responsible for introducing Paul to the other Apostles in the first place.

Barnabas is actually called an apostle at Lystra (Acts 14:14) – it should be noted that Paul and Luke use the word 'apostle' differently – and there is no doubt that his personal qualities and his faithful companionship to Paul gave him considerable standing among the early Christians. He is supposed to have founded the Cypriot Church, and according to a legend he was martyred at Salamis. Some writers identify him as one of the seventy (Luke 10:1), like Matthias. At any rate, he was clearly the kind of personality who could cope with Paul's energy and articulacy. Each doubtless depended on the other, but we may hazard a guess that Paul depended on him a great deal. Here is one more example of the disciplines and opportunities of working for the Kingdom of God in pairs.

Although Barnabas' name appears in the list of saints in the old Roman eucharistic prayer (sometimes called 'The Canon', because it was fixed) from the seventh century onwards, we do not encounter his commemoration in the calendar until the ninth century, in England, France and Germany. From there, like the other commemorations we have already observed, his date will have spread south to Rome and across the Western world. And as a thoroughly acceptable New Testament figure, he survived the Reformation into the Prayer Books, again like most of the commemorations we are looking at.

Today's Collect is a revision of that contained in *The Alternative Service Book (1980)*, with one or two hints of the old Prayer Book Collect. The Acts reading, almost invariably on this occasion in the past, tells of the Church in Antioch having Barnabas sent to them from Jerusalem, and of them seeing his 'steadfast purpose', 'full of the Holy Spirit and of faith' (Acts 11:19–30). Some of these qualities are reflected in the Old Testament reading (Job 29:11–16), and the epistle is one of the passages which mentions Barnabas as Paul's companion (Gal. 2:1–10). In line with other apostolic celebrations around this time of the year, the gospel reading is from the farewell discourses, and duplicates in part the passage chosen for Matthias the Apostle (14 May), although it is slightly shorter (John 15:12–17). It is the call to love one another, which, although obviously central to the Christian gospel, perhaps might have inspired a different passage from the same section. The Post-Communion Prayers are once more either from Pentecost in *The Alternative Service Book (1980)* or from the Canadian *Book of Alternative Services* (1985). Each is full of zeal to live the life of faith, in companionship and worship.

To be an agent of divine encouragement and consolation means, above all, a life of deep joy. Towards the end of the sixteenth century, Richard Hooker (*c.*1554–1600) wrote the following words about joy, and they are particularly appropriate to ponder today:

> The joy that setteth aside labour disperseth those things which labour gathereth. For gladness doth always rise from a kind of fruition and happiness, which happiness banisheth the cogitation of all want, it needeth nothing but only the bestowing of that it hath, inasmuch as the greatest felicity that felicity hath is to spread and enlarge itself.
>
> It cometh hereby to pass that the first effect of joyfulness is to rest, because it seeketh no more; the next, because it aboundeth, to give. The root of both is the glorious presence of that joy of mind which riseth from the manifold consider-ations of God's unspeakable mercy, into which considerations we are led by occasion of sacred times.

Richard Hooker, *Laws of Ecclesiastical Polity*, Vol. V, ch. 71.10.

The Birth of John the Baptist

24 June (Festival – White)

John the Baptist can be a somewhat daunting figure. Artists may try depict him as a rough and ready character. He wears camel skin and eats locusts and wild honey. When set alongside Jesus, he looks and appears awkward and different. He comes from an impeccable clerical background, on which he turns his back, in order to go out into the wilderness to preach a baptism of repentance and the Coming One. Jesus, on the other hand, is on the surface no more and no less than the son of an obscure carpenter, and exemplifies the virtues of traditional Jewish piety.

Here is a dilemma. How is it dealt with? Although John the Baptist appears in all four Gospels, and all four either allude to or recount his preaching, his baptism of Jesus, his eclipse by Jesus' public ministry and his beheading, it is once again Luke's Gospel which gives us the fullest portrait of all. Luke tells us of the 'Annunciation' of John's birth to his father in the Temple (Luke 1:5–25), the Visitation of Mary to Elizabeth (Luke 1:39–45), and the birth itself, followed by his father Zechariah's canticle, the Benedictus (Luke 1:57–79). This whole section ends with the telling verse which reveals that 'the child grew and became strong in Spirit, and he was in the wilderness until the day of his manifestation to Israel' (Luke 1:80). This sequence, carefully intertwined with the Annunciation to Mary, and intricately preceding the birth of Jesus in Bethlehem (Luke 2:1–7), is grist to Luke's mill which is to stress that the Forerunner of the Lord was born accordingly to God's plan, and that he did not stumble into a personal desire which took him out into the wilderness.

An angel, therefore, announces his birth to Zechariah who, unlike Mary, does not have faith and is therefore dumb until after his birth. In spite of this, John leaps in his womb as he recognizes the voice of the mother of his Lord. And then when he is born, he is given a name quite different from any name known in the family (an unconventional action that would symbolize discontinuity) and people begin to wonder what on earth he would be like. It is significant, too, that Zechariah's canticle comes after Mary's. Mary can sing of the glories of the Lord before her child has even been born, but Zechariah has to wait until after the birth, until after he has seen the awesome reaction of his neighbours to this infant born of an aged mother and given a name unprecedented in the lineage. The message that John preached was one of discontinuity with the values of the age.

We see nothing but contrasts, and contrasts continue, as Luke recounts John's preaching and his baptism of Jesus (Luke 3:1–22). Jesus' baptism is quite different from everyone else's even though Jesus is – according to Luke's account – among the people (Luke 3:21). Then, when John's disciples challenge Jesus about whether he is the Coming One or not, Jesus does not reply with teaching, but with what has *happened* – 'the blind receive their sight, the lame walk, lepers are cleansed, and the deaf hear, the dead are raised up, the poor have good news preached to them'. (Luke 7:18–23). Matthew and Mark, on the other hand, describe John's beheading in full (Matt. 14:1ff., Mark 6:14ff.), whereas Luke only alludes to it (Luke 9:7–9). He who has taken such care to give the details of the Baptist's birth, is reticent about his execution at Herod's hands. Another contrast.

When did today's festival, in all its isolated Lucan splendour, come to be commemorated in the Church? Its importance is to be found in the fact that like the Naming, the Epiphany, the Presentation in the Temple, the Annunciation, and Mark the Evangelist, this Festival has been kept today – in East *and* West – for a very long time indeed, since at least the second half of the fourth century. Augustine of Hippo refers to it as a 'great day'. In the next century, Maximus of Turin assumes that it is celebrated generally all over the West. In sixth-century Rome, it was so important that it was preceded by a fast and the Eucharist was celebrated in the Baptistery of St John the Lateran, Rome's cathedral.

The font is where we are reborn, we are washed, and we die and rise with Christ. Few people attending such a Eucharist could fail to pick up the important resonance with the Baptist's own death, for he who baptized Jesus was in effect the first martyr of the new dispensation. This is why Western iconography often depicts John the Baptist holding a reed with a suggestion of a cross at the top. All these contrasts reflect Jesus' own ringing verdict on his cousin, 'I tell you, among those born of women none is greater than John; yet he who is least in the Kingdom of God is greater than he' (Luke 27:28; Matt. 11:11). Luke who uniquely makes John a close relation keeps wanting to show how similar and yet how different they are.

The Collect for today goes back to the Prayer Book and before that to the Gregorian Sacramentary. The key word is 'providence', which reflects the Lucan implied accent on the divine purpose in preparing for John's birth. The Old Testament reading (Isa. 40:1−11) is perhaps one of the best known passages from Isaiah, from which all the Gospel writers quote in one way or another in their narratives of John's preaching in the wilderness (Matt. 3:3; Mark 1:3; Luke 3:4−6; John 1:23). The epistle teaches about faith and baptism, through which we have put on Christ (Gal. 3:23−9). The alternative reading (which may replace either Old Testament or epistle) is from Paul's speech in Antioch of Pisidia (Acts 13:14b−26), in which he mentions John's ministry of preaching the baptism of repentance to the people of Israel; in the course of this the Gospel writers are quoted when John himself says, 'What do you suppose that I am? I am not he, no, but after me one is coming, the sandals of whose feet I am not worthy to untie' (Matt. 3:11; Luke 3:16; John 1:20). And the gospel is Luke's narrative of the Baptist's birth, the Benedictus, and the final verse, which takes John into the wilderness (Luke 1:57–66, 80). The Post-Communion Prayer, a new composition, but in part inspired by an English translation of the new Roman text, draws the image of Jesus as the 'Lamb of God' (as John calls him, John 1:29), and moves from the sacramental feeding of forgiveness and life-giving love towards the discipleship that 'may ever tell of your mercy and your peace'.

In the early nineteenth century, Thomas Biddulph, (1763–1838) wrote as follows on today's feast:

> The Baptist's nativity is the only one (that of Christ excepted) which the church has thought proper to celebrate. The days appointed for the commemoration of other saints are generally those on which they respectively ceased from their labours and entered into their everlasting rest ... But the nativity of St John being designed, by the remarkable incidence that accompanied it, has turned the eyes of men towards one who is far greater – one, the latchet of whose shoes he confessed himself not worthy to unloose – the church keeps a day sacred to it, and directs us to begin our meditations by considering, as all Judea did when it happened, 'what manner of child' that should be, which was so wonderfully born (Luke 1:66).

> Thomas Biddulph, *Practical Essays on the Morning and Evening Services and on the Collects in the Liturgy of the Church of England*, Vol. III (London: Hatchard, 1822), pp. 356f.

Peter and Paul, Apostles / Peter the Apostle

29 June (Festival – Red)

Alternatives can be a little baffling at first. Today there is the choice of celebrating *either* Peter and Paul together, in accordance with a tradition going back in the East and West to the earliest times, *or* Peter alone, as in the first English Prayer Books. The reason for this latter provision is simple: at the Reformation, it was felt that Peter and Paul should have one day each, and that Paul's conversion was enough (25 January). Most modern revisions revert to the earlier practice, which makes a great deal of sense, so long as it does not lead us to forget Peter himself.

There can be little doubt that Peter was a dominant figure in the early Church. He keeps recurring in the Gospels, as one of the first to be called, as part of an 'inner cabinet' consisting of himself and the two sons of Zebedee, James and John, most notably at scenes like the Transfiguration (see 6 August). In the Acts of the Apostles, the first part is mainly devoted to Peter, and the second to Paul. Two Epistles bear his name, and the first contains no fewer than sixty Old Testament quotations, which suggests that Jewish origins shone through in a desire of the writer to show that the new religion had indeed superseded the old.

That pattern of the new taking over from the old is strongly reflected in two aspects of the Gospel narratives. First, for all that Peter is the hothead and impulsive character, that he denies Christ three times, John's Gospel also rehabilitates him (John 21:15ff.). Peter is held out as a figure with whom every fast-moving enthusiast can identify. He keeps getting it wrong, and Christ is still ready to forgive him.

Secondly, there is the central text which has always been read as the gospel for today, which is Matthew's account of Peter's confession of Christ at Caesarea Philippi. Jesus presses Peter to say who he is, to put into words how Peter perceives his identity. When he says, 'You are the Christ, the Son of the living God', Jesus calls him blessed, affirms that God had revealed this to him, changes his name from Simon to Peter (meaning the rock), and asserts that he will build his Church on this foundation. Although later ecclesiastical polemic clearly made a great deal of this text, much of it of an exaggerated kind, there can nonetheless be little doubt that Jesus saw in Peter a leader for the early Church, no more, no less. And although the 'keys of the Kingdom of Heaven' have been variously interpreted, the authority to bind and loose which is now given to him in the name of the whole Church indicates that the gospel community is not going to be based on vague ideas, but will have authority over people and their relationships, an authority which should be used responsibly.

The Gospel writers all tell of the calling of Peter (Matt. 4:18–20; Mark 1:16–18; Luke 5:1–11; John 1:35–42) in slightly different ways. Matthew and Mark are characteristically similar, placing it at the start of Jesus' ministry. Luke has it in the context of the miraculous catch of fish, when Jesus tells the fishermen to cast their nets after they had toiled all night. John, on the other hand, has Andrew his brother bring Peter to Christ. Here, then, is the person who takes over leadership of the disciples after the crucifixion, a leadership conceded by Paul himself (Gal. 1:18). Here, then, is the person who is three times arrested, according to the Acts of the Apostles (Acts 4:3; 5:18; 12:3). Here, then, is the man who delivers no fewer than *nine* speeches in that same book, perhaps an indication that he had a natural gift in this regard. Here, then, is the man who clashed with Paul over whether Gentile converts should be circumcised as well as baptized, and over missionary strategy.

Here, too, is the man who by tradition met his end by being crucified upside down in Rome – because he himself said that he was not worthy of being crucified the same way as Jesus –

and who together with Paul has been feasted on 29 June for centuries. All the indications are that this commemoration goes back to at least the fourth century, if not before then. There has been a shrine in the Vatican area since the second century, where Peter was buried. St Peter's Basilica, in its original form, was built during the time of Pope Sylvester (314–35) over the traditional site of Peter's tomb. It was repeatedly decorated and re-endowed with gifts by subsequent Popes, including Sergius I (687–701), the Syrian Pope who instigated the processions at the Marian feasts. And St Peter's came to be a site where Popes were buried. There was, too, an ancient basilica of St Paul's, built in the latter part of the fourth century, which was longer than St Peter's. It was burnt down in 1823, but rebuilt. Perhaps strangely, there is no tradition of what Peter looked like, unlike Paul (see 25 January). He is generally depicted with two keys, one gold and one silver, or else with a cock – the cock that crowed when Peter had twice denied Jesus (John 18:27).

Today's Collects are both new, based on those in *The Alternative Service Book (1980)*. That for Peter and Paul inserts a reference to unity ('made one by his Spirit'), in line with the traditional Latin Collect for today. The two basic readings for today, whichever option is taken, are those which have been used in the West for centuries, namely the narrative of Peter's third arrest (Acts 12:1–11) and Matthew's account of the confession of St Peter, with his change of name, and the foundation of the Church upon his ministry (Matt. 16:13–19). These are fundamental to the day, whether it is to be Peter and Paul, or Peter on his own. For Peter and Paul, the Old Testament reading is the vision of the seven lamps and two olive trees. The former are the eyes of the Lord that see everywhere, and the latter are 'the two anointed who stand by the Lord of the whole earth', which are interpreted as Peter and Paul themselves (Zech. 4:1–6a, 10b–14). If the Acts reading is read as the first lesson, the epistle reading is the well-known passage in 2 Timothy in which Paul commends himself to the Lord: 'I fought the good fight, I finished the race' (2 Tim. 4:6–8, 17–18). If Peter only is celebrated, the Old Testament lesson is the Ezekiel prophecy that the Lord will close and open his mouth (Ezek. 3:22–7). And if the Acts reading is the first lesson, then the epistle is Peter's warning that suffering will come the way of Christians, as with Christ himself (1 Pet. 2:19–25). The Post-Communion Prayers once more repeat the provision we have seen already, from Pentecost in *The Alternative Service Book (1980)*, or from the Canadian *Book of Alternative Services* (1985).

In his classic commentary on John's Gospel, B. F. Westcott (1825–1901) had this to say on Peter's call as a disciple:

> Unlike Philip he is confident, because he knows the strength of his love; unlike Thomas he is hopeful, because he knows whom he loves. But his confidence suggests the mode of his action: his hope fashions the form of its fulfilment. Peter saith unto Jesus, 'Thou shalt never wash my feet', and then with a swift reaction, 'Lord, not my feet only, but also my hands and my head' (John 13:6ff.). If he hears of a necessary separation, he asks, 'Lord, why can I not follow thee now? I will lay down my life for thy sake' (John 13:36ff.). He draws his sword in the garden (John 18:10f.): he presses into the courtyard with a High Priest (John 18:16ff.). He dares all and doubts nothing. But when the trial came he was vanquished by a woman. He had chosen his own part, and the bitterness of utter defeat placed him for ever at the feet of the saviour whom he had denied. He knew, though it was with grief, the meaning of the last triple charge: he knew, though it was through falls, the meaning of the answer to his last question: if I will that he tarry till I come, what is that to thee? Follow thou me (John 21:22).

B. F. Westcott, *The Gospel According to Saint John* (London: Murray, 1919), p. lxxiv.

Thomas the Apostle

3 July (Festival – Red)

Nicknames can be dangerous. And never more so than with Thomas the Apostle, who is often referred to as 'Doubting Thomas'. It casts a slur on an important witness to the resurrection, and has even made him seem a second-class disciple. It is as if the rest of the apostolic band were well ahead of him, with all the right answers, and their theological examinations suitably passed, leaving Thomas behind as a less than satisfactory figure.

As is often the case, the truth is more subtle. Although Thomas appears in the usual lists, it is in the Fourth Gospel that we find his personal development carefully worked out. This takes us to four significant passages. First, when Jesus receives the news that Lazarus has died, and says that he is glad, so that people can believe, Thomas says to his fellow disciples, 'Let us also go, that we may die with him' (John 11:16). Thomas shows that he is impulsive. He wants to go with Jesus on the journey, but he thinks it will end in his death. Secondly, in the Upper Room after the foot-washing, when Jesus has said to his disciples that they know where he is going, Thomas says, 'Lord, we do not know where you are going; how can we know the way?' (John 14:5). Thomas is cautious. He probably already feels that he has made a fool of himself and he wants to have a precise map before he starts the journey, an understandable attitude. Thirdly, there is the resurrection scene, when he arrives after the others, and insists that he must see for himself the print of the nails and be able to place his finger in their mark and Jesus' side (John 21:25). Eight days later, Thomas is with the other disciples, and through a closed door Jesus appears, and speaks directly to

Thomas, knowing his state of mind. Jesus is ready for Thomas to touch the wounds and that is enough in itself – 'My Lord and my God' (John 20:26ff.). Thomas is sceptical – then believing. Finally, Thomas is to be found among a group of disciples ready to go fishing, where once again they see the Lord (John 21:2ff.). Thomas is now faithful.

Each stage is important. From impulsiveness through caution to deep scepticism to faith. This is his personality, one which by temperament makes him ask questions that others are not prepared to ask. This is not the impulsiveness to do things that we saw in the case of Peter, but the impulsiveness to get at the truth. And many people continue to find themselves in Thomas, and they therefore do not like to see him sidelined and patronized, because he was honest and he was forthright. He ends up alongside Simon Peter and the other disciples on that dramatic fishing expedition at the end of John's Gospel as a result of a journey towards faith that was neither straightforward nor easy.

Thomas has been associated with South India from the very earliest times, and the 'Thomas Christians' there believe they can trace their Church right back to a mission by Thomas himself. Christians in Malabar have a special devotion to him, and they commemorate him on 3 July, as well as 18 and 21 December, just to make the point. He is supposed to have been buried at Milapore, near Madras, but his body was moved to Edessa in the year 394. Some think he is still buried in India. King Alfred the Great in the ninth century knew of India, and of Thomas' traditional place there. There is a tradition that 3 July was the date of his death. Such was the strength of his personal following that among the many legends written after the time of the New Testament, there were some attributed to Thomas himself. The *Acts of Thomas* even include the marriage of a couple, which Thomas as a wandering apostle stumbled upon, and a lengthy blessing is prised from him!

For some reason, 21 December was chosen as the day on which to feast him in the West, where he appears in calendars from the seventh century onwards. This is the date which is to be found in the Prayer Book. Following the Roman Catholic lead in the recent revisions, he was shifted to the traditionally even older date of 3 July, to prevent him being overshadowed by Christmas.

Today's Collect is a lightly revised version of *The Alternative Service Book (1980)* prayer, but now stresses our calling to confess Christ as our Lord and our God. (The Prayer Book Collect ended on the negative note, 'that our faith in thy sight may never be reproved'). The Old Testament reading depicts the watchman awaiting the time of his vision (Hab. 2:1–4). The epistle (which at one stage in the Middle Ages was used almost as an all-purpose epistle for the feasts of the apostles) exhorts us as no longer strangers and sojourners but fellow citizens with the saints, a dwelling place of God on the foundation of the apostles and prophets (Eph. 2:19–22). The gospel passage has always been read on this day, and it is the central passage of Thomas before Christ in the Upper Room after the resurrection (John 20:24–9). And the Post-Communion Prayers repeat the provision we have already come across for apostles and evangelists.

William Temple (1881–1944) wrote a series of meditations on the Fourth Gospel. This is what he has to say about Thomas in the Upper Room:

> He had demanded sight and touch; the Lord has offered himself to both; Thomas does not seek to touch. He has seen; that is enough ... Do you really suppose that the ground of your faith is your experience in this moment? No; of course not; it is grounded in that loyalty which made you ready to share your master's journey to death. This moment has done no more than release a faith which was ready, if it could find an occasion, to burst its inhibitions.

William Temple, *Readings in Saint John's Gospel* (London: Macmillan, 1952), p. 391.

Mary Magdalene

22 July (Festival – White)

Magadal (or Migdal) is a small town near Tiberius, in Galilee. Since there are a number of Marys in the New Testament, and she was neither the wife nor the mother of any known specific figure, the Mary of today's feast is invariably referred to as the Mary of Magadal, or Mary Magdalene.

All four Gospels tell us about her. In Matthew's Gospel, she is present at the crucifixion, and at the burial, and again by the tomb on Easter morning (Matt. 27:56–61; 28:1). In Mark's Gospel, we have the same sequence, but sharpened slightly. Mary 'beholds' the crucifixion, and the tomb, and she brings spices to the tomb (Mark 15:40,47; 16:1). In Luke, she is numbered among the women with Jesus (Luke 8:2) and she tells the apostles that the tomb is empty (Luke 24:10).

It is, however, in the Fourth Gospel that we have the most dramatic picture of all. She waits with the other women by the cross (John 19:25), but in the following chapter she has a central role. She comes alone to the tomb (in the other Gospels she is accompanied), and after Peter and John have been at the tomb and fled, she stands outside, sees two angels, and the unknown figure asks her why she weeps. She replies that 'they have taken away the Lord' and she does not know where they have laid him. The figure asks again why she is weeping and whom she seeks. She turns round and recognizes the unknown figure as her Master. The risen Christ tells her not to touch him. She goes and tells the disciples (John 20:1–2, 11–18).

Each of the four Gospels paints a different portrait. The passive but still active figure in Matthew is the 'beholding' figure in Mark, who brings spices. In Luke, she is a companion of Jesus who is ready to tell the disciples of the resurrection. But John's Gospel enables us to see by far the most dramatic transformation of all. That dialogue by the tomb with Christ turns her from being a dejected figure intent on doing her duty towards her dead loved one into a figure who recognizes through tear-filled eyes that the person she loved is somehow alive again. Her faith becomes obedient – she is not to touch and be dependent upon this apparition – and she goes and becomes part of the Easter community and tells the good news to others.

Mary goes on to become a favourite figure in art. But there is one sad twist to the tale. Gregory the Great, in one of his sermons, identifies her with the adulterous woman who washes Jesus' feet with her tears and dries them with her hair when he is at supper with friends (Luke 7:36–50). *That* particular anonymous figure is a fallen woman, who is rebuked by the other supper guests. By no coincidence, the gospel reading chosen for today in the Middle Ages was this passage, and it is reflected in the wooden statue by Donatello (*c.*1460) in the baptistery in the Museo del Duomo. She is a haggard and forsaken figure, suggesting rejection by those around her.

This may be why it took some time for her to enter the calendar – apostle of the Resurrection as she clearly is in the Fourth Gospel. We know that her relics are supposed to have been placed in a monastery in Constantinople in 899, and that she was commemorated in the calendar there in the tenth century. But she doesn't appear in Western calendars until the eleventh century at Rome, and her commemoration spreads from there. (This is the reverse of what we have seen in the case of some of the apostles, particularly the Conversion of St Paul, whose celebrations begin in north Europe, and from there spread south to Italy.) She is, therefore, a late entry into the calendar, and at the Reformation, she survives into the first Prayer Book of 1549, with a Collect and readings, but thereafter she appears only in the calendar, and loses the specific liturgical provision. Perhaps this mild survival is due to the fact that she has colleges dedicated to her at Oxford and Cambridge, and 187 ancient parish churches dedicated to her in England.

Today's Collect is adapted from *The Alternative Service Book (1980)* and is based on an older form. The Old Testament reading is a song to the beloved (S. of S. 3:1–4). The epistle, reflecting the focus of the new gospel reading, is a call to regard ourselves 'no longer from a human point of view' (2 Cor. 5:14–17). The most radical change follows the new revisions in the choice of gospel. This is no longer the medieval lesson (Luke 7:36–50), with its unsatisfactory and dubious identification of Mary with the fallen woman at Jesus' feet. We are now taken straight to the Easter tomb and read of the encounter between the risen Christ and Mary herself (John 20:1–2, 11–18). The Post-Communion Prayer is a new composition which relates that risen encounter to the eucharistic table: 'in your mercy, help us, who have been united with him in this eucharist, to proclaim the good news that he is alive and reigns, now and for ever'.

There have been many famous Easter sermons, but perhaps the most famous of all on this text was preached by Lancelot Andrewes (1555–1626) in 1619 before the Court of James I. In typical fashion, he muses deeply and at length, intuitively and imaginatively, on the scene in the garden that Easter morning as depicted by the Fourth Gospel. Here he describes the transforming Easter faith:

Well now, he that was thought lost is found again: and found, not as he was sought for, not a dead body, but a living soul; nay, a quickening spirit then. And that might Mary Magdalene well say. He showed it, for he quickened her and her spirits, that were as good as dead. You thought you should have come to Christ's resurrection day and so you do. But not to his alone, but even to Mary Magdalene's resurrection too. For in very deed, a kind of resurrection it was, was wrought in her; revived, as it were and raised from the dead and drooping, to a lively and cheerful estate. The gardener had done his part, made her all green on the sudden.

Lancelot Andrewes, *Ninety-Six Sermons of Lancelot Andrewes*, Library of Anglo-Catholic Theology (Oxford: Parker, 1841) Vol. III, p. 21.

James the Apostle

25 July (Festival – Red)

When the German occupying forces left Denmark at the end of the Second World War, my father was serving as a military intelligence officer in the British Army. Among the many papers which had been left behind that he had to scrutinize was a list of 'prominenti', who were on a 'hit list' and liable to be taken out and executed summarily, if the circumstances required. Among those, on one list, was the Bishop of Aarhus. This caused my father wry amusement later on, as he married the Bishop's daughter! The good Bishop lived on to serve his diocese for many further years, and his grandson took his funeral in 1979.

The execution of 'prominenti' is a constant ingredient in the history of the human race, whether or not matters of religion become part of the equation. Today's feast commemorates James the Apostle, the brother of John, part of that 'inner cabinet' with Simon Peter who are particularly close to Jesus. He was the first apostle to die for the Christian faith, as today's reading from Acts tells us (Acts 11:27–12:2). He was executed under orders from King Herod Agrippa in AD 44. Although dying for the Christian faith became part of the life of the early Church, indeed a great force for solidarity, this particular death must have held an important place both at the time and thereafter. James heads the list of prominent Church leaders who have been picked out by insecure political leaders, because they feel that the system that they represent is being undermined unduly by their mere existence. Such a pattern of things has run into the twentieth century, as witness the martyrdoms of Janani Luwum, the Anglican Archbishop of Uganda, in 1977, and of

Oscar Romero, the Roman Catholic Archbishop of San Salvador, in 1980.

The Gospels of Matthew, Mark and Luke tell us something of the story of James' following of Christ, but it is Mark's Gospel which gives us the fullest picture. We can, therefore, with some accuracy regard this particular festival as Marcan. All three tell us of his call (Matt. 4:21; Mark 1:19; Luke 5:10), of his being numbered among the apostles (Matt. 10:2; Mark 3:17; Luke 6:14) and of his being present at the Transfiguration (Matt. 17:1; Mark 9:2; Luke 9:18). But Mark adds more. James goes to the house of Simon and Andrew after their call by Jesus (Mark 1:29). He also goes with Peter at the raising of Jairus' daughter (Mark 5:37 – also added by Luke, 8:51). But there are three important additional appearances of James in the Marcan account.

First of all, James and his brother John ask for ringside seats in the Kingdom of Heaven (Mark 10:35,41). It is significant that *they* ask him, not their mother, as in Matthew's Gospel (Matt. 19:28), nor in a general dispute among the disciples after the Last Supper as in Luke (Luke 22:22–24:30). In Mark's Gospel, James and his brother John come *direct*.

Secondly, James and John and the other two brothers Peter and Andrew ask Jesus privately at the Mount of Olives, 'When will all this be?' – the coming of the Kingdom, when all is accomplished. Jesus replies with a warning that 'many will come' in his name and that they must 'take heed' for themselves (Mark 13:5,9).

Finally, in the loneliness of the Garden of Gethsemane, he leaves the disciples, but takes Peter and James and John to pray with him, where he was 'greatly distressed and troubled' (Mark 14:33). This inner cabinet shares in Christ's sorrow and spiritual agony. And it is one of these, James the Apostle, often referred to as 'James the Great', whom King Herod Agrippa executed with the sword at Passover time, going on to arrest Peter, because it pleased the Jews (Acts 12:1–3).

It was inevitable that he should find a place in the Christian calendar, given such a prominent death. Because he was killed at Passover time, in the Coptic and Byzantine traditions he is celebrated on 12 and 30 April respectively. There was also a tradition of celebrating him together with his brother John after the Nativity of Christ, to express their kinship as 'Sons of Thunder'. From the seventh century, his cult takes hold in the West. His supposed relics were moved from Jerusalem and deposited in Compostella, on the site of an early Christian cemetery, which is where a saint in early patristic times whose name is unknown was obviously buried. This 'translation' of his relics is first attested only in the year 865, by which time he was well established in Western calendars on 25 July.

Compostella was renamed Santiago (i.e. Saint James) da Compostella and became a pilgrimage centre in the later Middle Ages, fostered by kings and church leaders. He is often represented by a shell, a pilgrim's emblem, as a result of his popularity among pilgrims travelling to Compostella. It is possible that his relics were deposited there even before the year 627, as a bulwark against the Islamic invasion of Spain which began that year, and which had such a strong impact on Western Europe. James was a popular dedication in this country, and 400 churches were dedicated to him in medieval England.

The Collect for this day goes back to the Prayer Book, and stresses James following Christ 'without delay'. The reading for the epistle, also from the Prayer Book (but surprisingly not used in the Middle Ages), is the central narrative of James' martyrdom (Acts 11:27–12:2). The Old Testament reading in use in the modern revisions is the 'Word for Baruch', warning Jeremiah not to seek great things for himself (Jer. 45:1–5). When the Acts reading is read first, and there is an epistle, the modern Roman Catholic provision is followed in Paul's well-known image of the treasure in earthenware vessels (2 Cor. 4:7–15), eminently suitable for the first martyr apostle. The gospel passage, part of which has been read on this day in the West for centuries, is the parable of the labourers in the vineyard (Matt. 20:20–8). And the Post-Communion Prayers once more repeat the provision in *The Alternative Service Book (1980)* for Pentecost, emphasizing boldness to preach the gospel, or that of the 'apostles' teaching and fellowship' in the Canadian *Book of Alternative Services* (1985).

James' life and death bring us close to the the real cost of discipleship. He was among the first to be called by Christ. He was among the first to die for him. And he died just because he was a prominent Christian leader who would give satisfaction to those intent on persecuting the new faith. He was, above all, one of the children of light, and the following words from a sermon preached in St Margaret's Westminster some years ago by John Austin Baker (1928-) take us to the centre of the Christian faith:

> We need the light, the full daylight on our lives, to judge and correct us. The more openly we live, the more likely we are to discern our own faults and to shape our conduct by standards that are worthy and true . . . For when the ingredients of our life are placed in the full light of day, then they do indeed in their turn enlighten our souls to the truth.
>
> John Austin Baker, *The Whole Family of God* (London: Mowbrays, 1981), p. 21.

The Transfiguration of Our Lord

6 August (Festival – White or Gold)

Mountaineering is not everyone's way to relax, but people who have climbed to the top of a hill together often convey to friends and relatives afterwards what an experience it was. Anyone who lived in the Holy Land at the time of Christ would have been familiar with hill climbing, whether in the south, in Judea, where the shepherds looked after their flocks by night at the birth of Christ, or in the north, to either side of Galilee, where today's commemoration of the Transfiguration of our Lord may well have its geographical origins.

But what did happen? Matthew, Mark and Luke all give similar accounts. Significantly, the Fourth Gospel does not, but its perspective on the life of Christ has its own dimensions of glory and 'transfiguration' so that this kind of event might seem superfluous. Mark's account is a full one (Mark 9:1–9). Jesus took Peter, James and John to a high mountain; this was identified by Cyril of Jerusalem in the fourth century as Mount Tabor, but it is more likely to be one of the three spurs of Mount Hermon, which is about nine thousand feet high and overlooks Caesarea Philippi. Jesus is transfigured before them and his garments become white, and Elijah and Moses appear and talk with him. Peter becomes so enthused that he wants to make three tabernacles, one for Jesus, and one for Moses, and one for Elijah. Peter, not for the first time, got things wrong. God's 'tabernacling', God's dwelling with humanity, no longer depends upon building a shrine, but on the presence of Jesus himself. At this point a cloud overshadows them and a voice comes out of the cloud identifying Jesus as his beloved son, whom the disciples must *hear*. Then suddenly they saw no-one any more, except Jesus and themselves. The experience was over.

Matthew's account follows Mark closely, as we come to expect (Matt. 17:1–9), but there are small additions. Jesus' face shines as the sun and a bright cloud overshadows the disciples. Matthew wants to draw attention to the parallel of Jesus going up this mountain and Moses going to Mount Sinai, so the voice from the cloud makes the disciples afraid. Jesus frees them from that fear.

Luke's account is considerably different. He does not use the word 'transfigure', perhaps because of the audience he is considering which might misunderstand. As Jesus prays (a priority for Jesus in Luke's Gospel) his face is altered and his clothes are white and dazzling; Moses and Elijah appear in glory with him and they tell him about his 'departure', which he was to accomplish at Jerusalem. By linking this experience with Christ's prayer and his passion, Luke comes near to the Fourth Gospel where Christ's glory is found even when he offers himself to the Father in prayer before his death (John 17).

The new Roman sequence of readings following the revisions after the Second Vatican Council regards this festival as having such importance that the three accounts of the Transfiguration are read in the three-year cycle, following the Sunday lectionary. In the Middle Ages, however, Matthew's account was always used, reflecting the prominence given to Matthew's Gospel in Eucharist readings generally, and also following the Byzantine rite to this day. However, modern Anglican revisions tend to opt for the Lucan narrative, with all its individualities, because the Transfiguration is now part of the three-year Sunday cycle, either before or during Lent. Interestingly, when Mark Frank, the great figure of the seventeenth century, preached on this festival, he used the Lucan account as his text, at a time when the Transfiguration only survived in the Prayer Book calendar as a feast in name, but had no Collect or readings.

We are still left with a question, what actually happened up there? The master and his three closest followers climb a mountain together at a time of growing public interest in the meaning of this man's life and teaching. They go on a walk together to get away from everybody and everything. What ensues cannot be put into words and cannot be reconstructed historically. From the similarities of the three accounts as well as their differences, it is clear that something overwhelming did take place which was important for both Jesus himself and for Peter, James and John. It became so important for the early Christians that in the second Epistle that bears Peter's name, reference is made to witnessing the glory on the mountain (2 Pet. 1:16–19) – invariably the epistle for this day.

But how did the feast itself originate? We know that a church was built on Mount Tabor in the fourth century and that its dedication was on 6 August and it is an important festival in all the Eastern churches today, on the same level of importance as Christmas, Epiphany, Ascension and Pentecost. But the strange truth is that it took a long time for the Transfiguration to appear in the West. The Matthew account of Transfiguration appears as the gospel passage on a weekday in Lent – the Saturday before the second Sunday in Lent, to be precise! – in the early Middle Ages. From the eleventh and twelfth centuries, however, the feast itself starts appearing, with its epistle (2 Pet. 1:15–19) and the Matthew narrative (Matt. 17:1–9). Peter the Venerable, who died in 1156, was Abbot of the prestigious Abbey of Cluny. He emphasized that it was a great feast; and Pope Callixtus III extended its use throughout the West in 1457 after the defeat of the Turks at Belgrade the previous year. But, as we have already pointed out, it only appears in the Prayer Book among the calendar dates, and has no liturgical provision, although these began to reappear unofficially from the nineteenth century onwards, in line with the recovery of older traditions that has been such a mark of recent church history.

The Collect for today is new, revising *The Alternative Service Book (1980)* prayer with the important Lucan echo ('and spoke of the exodus he would accomplish at Jerusalem'). The Old Testament reading takes us to Daniel's vision, of 'one that was

ancient of days' and whose 'raiment was white as snow' (Dan.
7:9–10, 13–14); the epistle we have already mentioned (2 Pet.
1:16–19), as well as the Lucan narrative as the gospel (Luke
9:28b–36). The Post-Communion Prayer is from the Canadian
Book of Alternative Services (1980): like the Collect it begins
with the glory of Christ and moves through daily discipleship
to the Kingdom of Heaven itself.

Iconography of the Transfiguration abounds in glory! Christ is
usually depicted in the centre in a ray of light. Moses and Elijah,
representing Christ's continuity and discontinuity with the
priestly and prophetic traditions of the Old Testament, are often
on either side of him. The disciples are gathered into the scene,
as, indeed, is the onlooker as worshipper. Perhaps it was with
such iconographic perspectives in mind that Michael Ramsey
(1904–88), who loved preaching and teaching about the glory
and the suffering that unite in the figure of Christ, had this to
say about Transfiguration:

> Confronted as he is with a Universe more than ever terrible
> in the blindness of its processes and the destructiveness of its
> potentialities mankind must be led to the Christian faith not
> as a panacea of progress nor as an otherworldly solution
> unrelated to history, but as a Gospel of Transfiguration. Such
> a Gospel both transcends the world and speaks to the immedi-
> ate here-and-now. He who was transfigured is the Son of
> Man; and, as He discloses on Mount Hermon another world,
> He reveals that no part of created things and no moment of
> created time lies outside the power of the Spirit, who is Lord,
> to change from glory into glory.

> A. M. Ramsey, *The Glory of God and the Transfiguration of Christ*,
> Libra Books (London: Darton, Longman & Todd, 1967), p. 147.

The Blessed Virgin Mary

15 August (Festival – White or Gold)

The Virgin Mary is understandably one of the most frequent
figures in Christian art. She can be portrayed as the prayerful
and beautiful figure at the Annunciation. She can be the joyful
mother at the Nativity scene. She can be the Woman of Sorrows
standing by the cross. Or she can be a combination of all three.
When I was on holiday in Crete as a student, I went into an
antique souvenir shop in a small town and bought a modern
copy of an icon of Mary holding Jesus. The two are clearly in
close relationship with each other. But Jesus is no baby clutched
close to his mother's breast. He is rather a person in his own
right, holding a scroll representing his future ministry, and his
head is deliberately larger than natural proportions would allow.
Once, an Orthodox priest came to see me and I said to him,
'Look, here is my icon of the Virgin and Child.' Quick as a
flash, he gently corrected me: 'No, that is *not* what we call it in
the East. For us, that is an icon of the Incarnation.'

Would that many Western Christians had that sense of pro-
portion about the Virgin Mary. There are times when we seem
to be divided into two opposing camps. These consist of an
exaggerated Catholic view, which places Mary in such an
exalted place in the scheme of redemption that she almost
becomes a fourth member of the Trinity. On the other side,
there is an extreme Protestant view, that in counter-reaction
would really like to forget that she ever existed, save for the
fact that she was around at Bethlehem at the right time. Clearly
neither view will do. Nor does either view fully reflect the meaning of Scripture.

Matthew and Luke make much more of her over and above the simple fact of her giving birth to Jesus. Matthew takes care to point out that she conceived Jesus by the Holy Ghost, and Luke makes even more of her place in the unfolding life of Christ (see 2 February and 25 March). The Fourth Gospel, however, does not record Christ's birth in the same way at all, but 'the mother of Jesus' was present at the Wedding in Cana of Galilee (John 2:1ff.). And as Jesus hangs dying on the cross, he commends Mary to John, the disciple whom he loved, and John to Mary, in those memorable words, 'Woman, behold, your son' and 'Behold, your mother' (John 19:26f.). Here is Jesus founding the new community, the community of faith. It is not enough to be related to him because what is central is that he commits each one of us to the other. All family relationships, crucial and important as they are, have to take second place to this radically new criterion of discipleship. We are all inseparable from the figure of Christ, so it is not a case of us and Christ, but rather (to borrow words from St Paul) 'Christ in you, the hope of glory' (Col. 1:27).

We cannot look at Mary without considering what she did: she brought Christ into the world, she watched him die and she becomes part of the Easter community. It is surely this truth which inspired Elizabeth Frink's magnificently mobile-looking statue of the Virgin Mary which stands outside Salisbury Cathedral. Here is an older Mary, striding away from the tomb, to help create the new community. Curiously, although there was a time when Western Catholic piety did give the Virgin Mary an unduly prominent place, the older tradition of the Western Church was to keep only one festival in her honour, namely on 1 January, happily chosen so that the Nativity of Christ forms the essential background. But this was replaced in the seventh century by four festivals: the Presentation in the Temple (2 February), the Annunciation (25 March), and two others which mark the end and the beginning of her earthly life, namely the Assumption (15 August) and her Nativity (8 September). One can see a certain logic in the desire to celebrate such feasts. But what is the meaning of the Assumption, which is closely linked to today for many Christians?

The Assumption starts life in the legendary 'Lives of the Virgin Mary' that circulated in the early centuries. First of all, she is believed to have died and her body preserved and taken into heaven. Then she was regarded as having fallen asleep only, and her body thereafter assumed into heaven. The final stage is that she was taken straight to heaven without falling asleep at all. The notion of falling asleep, often translated as 'dormition', remains the title for this day's feast in Eastern Christianity, in contrast to Assumption, the more explicit title in the Roman Church.

People either take easily to these niceties or they find them hard to fathom. The best way to understand them is to ask why they arose in the first place. The process just described of moving from the assumption of her dead but preserved body into heaven, through assumption of a body that has fallen asleep, to assumption of a live body at the point of death, took place in Eastern Christianity in the late fifth and sixth centuries. It became essential to demonstrate to fashions which wanted to spiritualize Christ out of all natural existence that he was indeed born of a woman, into human history, at a specific time and in a specific place (precisely the concerns of Luke's narrative (Luke 2:1ff.), and that Christ's entering human history brought redemption to those who believe in him; and the first of the redeemed was regarded as Mary herself, whom the angel hailed as blessed (Luke 1:28).

All these different theories and explanations have as their background the definition made by the Councils of Ephesus (431) and Chalcedon (451) that the Virgin Mary should be called the 'Godbearer' (*Theotokos* in the Greek). Christ was both human and divine. If he was entirely human, then he could not redeem. If he was entirely divine, and did not truly enter the human condition, his redemption would not take on the full load of our human nature. And from that central truth, all those closest to him, the first among the communion of saints, are touched in an ever-increasing ray – which includes us as well. When we come to think of the Virgin Mary, we have to give her her due place. When we are dealing with the language of devotion, we have to realize that this is sometimes the language of poetry rather than of precise definition.

We have travelled to Jerusalem frequently as we consider the development of the Christian calendar, and it so happens that we know that in the fifth century, there was already at Jerusalem a festival of the Virgin Mary as the 'Theotokos', which was an all-embracing celebration akin to the old commemoration on 1 January in the West that was mentioned earlier. The readings were the prophecy of Isaiah that a virgin should conceive (Isa. 7:10–15), our status as God's children thanks to the birth of God's Son, born of a woman (Gal. 3:29–4:7) and the birth of Jesus (Luke 2:1–7).

It is this spirit of an all-embracing feast of the Virgin Mary that recent Anglican (and other) revisions seek to express today, without making a commitment to any specific understanding of Assumption, which, after all, was only proclaimed as dogma in the Roman Catholic Church as recently as 1950. Understandably, at the Reformation the festival of the Assumption did not survive into any of the Anglican or Lutheran calendars. And in our quest, we have been assisted by the older and more general approach to the commemoration of this day, and to the gentler and more iconographic tradition in Eastern Christianity, where 15 August soon came to be kept as the Dormition of the Virgin Mary, a celebration of the first of the redeemed, a redemption in which we all hope to share.

Today's Collect is a revision of *The Alternative Service Book (1980)* prayer with some material from the South African provision for this day. For the Old Testament, there is a choice between Isaiah prophesying exaltation in the garments of salvation, and righteousness springing forth before all the nations (Isa. 61:10–11) or John's vision of the woman appearing in heaven (Rev. 11:19–12:6,10). The gospel is, appropriately enough, the Song of Mary, the Magnificat (Luke 1:46–55). The

Post-Communion Prayer, another fine composition for a Marian feast, gives thanks for the visit of the Holy Spirit and his over-shadowing in the sacrament, and asks for strength 'to walk with Mary the joyful path of obedience'.

There is, in spite of Reformation controversies, a strand of conti-nuity in Anglican thought that is discernible in the writing of such seventeenth-century divines as Lancelot Andrewes, Jeremy Taylor and Mark Frank. One writer who is only this century receiving the attention he deserves is Thomas Traherne. He was a parish priest and a poet, who was born in Hereford in about 1636 and died in 1674. In one of his compositions, he describes the Virgin Mary as follows:

> The most illustrious light in the Church, wearing over all her beauties the veil of humility to shine the more resplendently in thy eternal glory.

> And yet this Holy Virgin mother styled herself as the hand-maid of the Lord, and falls down with all the glorious hosts of angels, and with the armies of saints, at the foot of thy throne, to worship and glorify thee for ever and ever.

> I praise thee O Lord with all the powers and faculties of my soul; for doing in her all thy merciful works for my sake, and the benefit of mankind.

> Quoted from A. M. Allchin, *The Joy of All Creation: An Anglican Meditation on the Place of Mary*, 2nd edition (London: Darton, Long-man & Todd, 1993), p. 118.

Bartholomew the Apostle

24 August (Festival – Red)

Bartholomew is the patron saint of butchers and he is often depicted with a butcher's knife because according to an early Christian tradition he was flayed alive in Albanopolis in Armenia. He is also the patron saint of tanners and all who work on skins, as an extension of that fateful knife ordeal. All this probably explains the dedication of St Bartholomew the Great in Smithfield, London, near the old meat market. Christian history, however, applies the butcher's knife in a particularly bloody form to the tragic side of the Reformation story in the St Bartholomew's Day massacre in 1572, when French Protestants (Huguenots) were put to death by Roman Catholics. This is not how the spirit of Bartholomew lives on, and as these painful wounds are slowly healed, we do well to see martyrdom as bearing witness to the truth of Christ in an alien world, with all the cost that *that* can bring, rather than as a way of explaining how Christians happen to fall out with each other, as we often and inevitably do. Other traditions connect him with India, where he is supposed to have left behind the Gospel according to Matthew in Hebrew. But saints can be ubiquitous figures, as we have already seen, and there is a church of St Bartholomew on the River Tiber in Rome that is supposed to have some of his relics.

But who was Bartholomew? He appears in all the lists of the apostles (Matt. 10:3; Mark 3:18; Luke 6:14; Acts 1:13) but nothing more is heard of him. Some scholars link him with Nathanael, the friend of Philip to whom Philip went and said, 'We have found him of whom Moses in the Law and also the

Prophets wrote, Jesus of Nazareth, the Son of Joseph,' which prompted the scathing question from Nathanael, 'Can anything good come out of Nazareth?' (John 1:45,46). The same Nathanael was among those disciples who gathered at Tiberias after the resurrection (John 21:1ff.). This is why the revised Roman Lectionary gives this particular narrative as the gospel for today (John 1:45–51). Probably because Bartholomew was not among the first rank of apostles, it took some time for him to enter the Christian calendar. We first encounter him in the West in the Sacramentaries of the eighth century in France, and his fame spread subsequently.

The Collect for today goes back to the Prayer Book, which is itself based on an older Latin original, particularly in the petition that 'your Church may love that word which he believed and may faithfully preach and receive the same'. The Acts reading tells of ministry in the early Church (Acts 5:12–16). If that is read as the second reading, we hear a prophecy that the blind will see and the deaf will hear for the Lord's work cannot be hindered (Isa. 43:8–13); otherwise the epistle has Paul describing the apostles as 'last of all . . . a spectacle to the world' (1 Cor. 4: 9–14). Modern Anglican choice for the gospel is also that of the medieval lectionaries, Christ's warning at the Last Supper to the disciples, who are disputing who among them was the greatest, that those who serve at table are greater than those who sit; the disciples are called to 'continue with me in my trials' (Luke 22:24–30). The Post-Communion Prayer is once more the choice of the two prayers, either from Pentecost in *The Alternative Service Book (1980)*, or from the Canadian *Book of Alternative Services* (1985) – boldness to preach the gospel, or the apostles' teaching and fellowship.

'Can anything good come out of Nazareth?' (John 1:46). This is the question Nathanael asks, and whether or not he was indeed Bartholomew, it points to a struggle that everyone who tries to follow Christ has to undergo, namely the struggle to come to terms with oneself. That means our capacity not only to believe in Christ but to believe in ourselves. In one of his many sermons, the great late nineteenth-century preacher and theologian H. P. Liddon (1829–90) preaches on words taken from today's gospel:

> Of St Bartholomew the Apostle himself little is known ... He is remembered ... in the Gospel, as one of the twelve among whom on the eve of the Passion there had been a strife which should be accounted the greatest. This last is the point which I invite you to consider this afternoon. For it is a help to us, my brethren, – to you and to me, – to remember that the Apostles of Christ did not become all at once what they were eventually. They had to struggle with weakness and errors of a fallen nature, just as we have. Like us, they had to curb temper and to check ambition; they did not begin by sitting on thrones, judging the twelve tribes of Israel; they carried their treasure full many a year in earthen vessels, that the excellency of their glory might be of God, and not themselves.

H. P. Liddon, *Sermons on Some Words of Christ* (London: Longmans, 1890), pp. 296f.

Holy Cross Day

14 September (Festival – Red)

On 21 March 1982, my father and I spent an unforgettable Sunday morning in the Church of the Holy Sepulchre in Jerusalem. We were in Israel for a week, to celebrate his sixty-eighth birthday, which we had done two days previously by driving up the Jordan Valley and round Galilee to Tiberias, where we sat at a lakeside restaurant and ate 'Peter fish', washed down with Mount Carmel wine. It was with some sense of anticipation that Sunday morning that we entered that ancient church on the site of where Christ is supposed to have been buried. Several different Christian Churches have rights over different parts of the building. The Copts have a little chapel on the other side of Christ's tomb. The Syrian Orthodox, worshipping in Aramaic, use another but larger space not far away. Suddenly the Roman Catholics entered for a somewhat Italianate-looking celebration. Finally, the Greek Orthodox celebrated what was for them the third Sunday in Lent, in a liturgy which ended in a procession with the Patriarch carrying a supposed relic of the true cross three times around the tomb.

As we watched this particular part of the service, and the two deacons walking backwards censing the relic enthusiastically, to the accompaniment of the strong melodies of Greek liturgical chant, both my father and I had a sense of not quite being where we were. We could not believe that we were in Jerusalem, near if not exactly over such very ancient sacred sites, in the presence of diverse liturgical traditions, which together have produced so many riches for Christianity, and for the whole of human civilization. Whatever exactly was in the Patriarch's hands, a true relic or not, we were so close to the heart of the Christian gospel, the cross itself, and we were in the midst of a spiritual tradition which both of us admired for different reasons, but in the presence of which we still felt somewhat alien. We were transported for a moment of eternity into heaven itself.

The cross belongs to all of us, but it took root in Palestine that first Good Friday when a young Galilean preacher was executed in a way that was both common and disgraceful at the time. All four Gospels are at one in giving a central place in the narrative to the passion of Christ, and while there are differences between one writer and another, all agree that the cross is at the centre of the Christian faith. When, a few centuries on, Christians emerged from the time of persecution and were able to express their life and worship much more publicly than before, Jerusalem naturally became a place where churches could be built to commemorate the events of the life of Christ. On 13 September 335, two churches side by side were dedicated, where Christ was crucified and buried respectively. The first church was called the Martyrium ('place of witness') and the second the Anastasis ('resurrection'). On the day after, the wood of the cross which had supposedly been discovered by Empress Helena, mother of the Emperor Constantine, was presented to the people to venerate, in the way that the nun Egeria who travelled from France or Spain on an extended holiday saw the same practice on Good Friday some time in the years between 381 and 386. It was always important – and remains so – to emphasize the historical and geographical truth of Christianity, which is not a passing philosophical fashion, but a series of interpretations of events that took place in a particular place and at a particular time, regardless of whether the calendar and the location are 100 per cent accurate.

This relic of the cross was captured by the Persians in the year 615 when they invaded Jerusalem, but it was returned after their subsequent defeat in the year 627, when the Emperor Heraclitus defeated the Persians himself. From that year onwards, 14 September, the day after the dedication festival in

Jerusalem, was kept as the feast of the exaltation of the cross. Later that century, when Sergius I was Pope (687–701), he showed his own enthusiasm for things Eastern that we have already seen in the Marian feasts by introducing the custom of the veneration of another relic of the cross in St Peter's. Among the prayers that were composed for this festival when it was first introduced at Rome is an offertory prayer (no longer used) at the Eucharist which prays that we may both adore and taste the full glory of the *banner* of the cross of Christ. Such military imagery reflects the famous opening of a Passiontide hymn by Venantius Fortunatus which begins, 'The royal banners onward go . . .' (This hymn was written specially in Poitiers in the 560s when a fragment of the true cross arrived in the city from Constantinople.) Fashions in language change, but the point of such imagery is to draw the contrast between physical warfare and carrying Christian convictions to their most appropriate level.

Whatever the appropriateness of this image, the notion that in the Eucharist we can adore the banner of the cross somehow brings today's festival to a powerful sacramental focus. It was bound to spread throughout the West as the dramatic political upheavals of the seventh century unfolded, with the relic stolen in 615 and restored in 627 and the festival taking root at Rome later on. Jerusalem's dedication festival in September by chance provided much of Christendom with the opportunity to celebrate the Holy Cross at a distance from Holy Week. At the Reformation, the festival survived in name only in the calendar. But it has been reintroduced in Anglican books in recent times, first informally and unofficially, and more recently in the era of liturgical revision. Today's Collect is that contained in *The Alternative Service Book (1980)*, which is itself adapted from one which was in circulation in Anglican books in the 1920s. The Old Testament reading is the brazen serpent in the wilderness (Num. 21:4–9). The epistle is the early Christian hymn of the humility and exaltation of Christ (Phil. 2:6–11). The gospel passage is part of Christ's words to Nicodemus, when he likens Moses lifting up the serpent in the wilderness to the Son of Man being lifted up so that 'whoever believes in Him may have eternal life' (John 3:13–17). The medieval Roman gospel reading was Christ's words about judgement and the ruler of this world being cast out (John 12:31–6), which was also in *The Alternative Service Book (1980)*. But the new sequence of readings is more coherent, particularly the relationship between the Old Testament and the gospel. The Post-Communion Prayer is taken from the Canadian *Book of Alternative Services* (1985), and reflects on the sacrament as a showing forth of the death of the Lord until he comes (1 Cor. 11:26).

The cross continues to fascinate Christians. There is no limit, it seems, to the extent to which it inspires artists, whether they are painting or composing music – or writing poetry. In the first half of the seventeenth century, John Donne (1571/2–1631) was one of the most influential figures in the English Church. He preached memorable sermons and wrote poems that are both passionate and meticulous. Here is the second part of one of his 'Divine Poems' entitled 'Crucifying':

> Loe, where condemned hee,
> Beares his owne crosse with paine, yet by and by
> When it beares him, he must beare more and die.
> Now thou art lifted up, draw mee to thee,
> And at thy death giving such liberall dole
> Moyst, with one drop of thy blood, my dry soule.

John Donne, *Complete Poems and Selected Prose*,
ed. John Hayward (London: Nonesuch, 1930), p. 278.

Matthew, Apostle and Evangelist

21 September (Festival – Red)

St Matthew's Church, Roslin, is one of the most extraordinary church buildings to survive the Reformation in Scotland. It was built in the late fifteenth century in extravagantly decorative Portuguese Gothic, which even to an untrained eye looks more Portuguese than Scottish. The building was never completed; all that we have is the part of the church intended for the college of clergy who gathered there for the daily services. This makes an ideal size of building for relatively small congregations to meet in a space that combines intimacy with grandeur.

I used to attend this church from time to time as a teenager and on one occasion was asked to read the second lesson at Evensong on the Sunday after Saint Matthew's Day. Because not many people in the congregation had been able to attend the Eucharist on the Festival itself, the gospel for Saint Matthew's Day was what I was given to read – the calling of Matthew from the receipt of custom to follow Christ, which has always been read on this day in all churches, Eastern as well as Western (Matt. 9:9–13). I particularly remember struggling through the final verse, Jesus' rebuke to those Pharisees who were complaining that he was sitting at table with tax collectors and sinners: 'Go and learn what this means, 'I desire mercy, and not sacrifice.' For I came not to call the righteous, but sinners' (Matt. 9:13). I enjoyed the Old Testament quotation, in which the prophet Hosea challenges the people to ensure that their lives match up to the high ideals expressed in their worship, 'I desire mercy, and not sacrifice' (Hosea 6:6). It is a quotation put into the mouth of Jesus in the same Gospel when Jesus is similarly challenged again (Matt. 12:7). But I found it a little hard to realize the full implications of the deliberate irony in the words, 'I came not to call the righteous, but sinners.'

And yet this is such a strong gospel truth, and a truth that is doubly appropriate in the context. Matthew is a tax collector, and therefore someone to whom the Roman occupying forces have subcontracted the gathering of their taxes, so that they can themselves subcontract another ingredient in the process, namely Jewish distrust of a fellow Jew who is now virtually a paid official of the Roman imperial administration. Matthew is a collaborator, and collaborators are seldom popular with self-styled zealous patriots.

But was this Matthew the author of the Gospel that bears his name? An early Christian writer named Papias, who also tells us that Mark was close to Peter, refers to Matthew as a collector of the sayings of Christ. Scholarly debate continues on this kind of question, and rightly so, but we can cautiously conclude that if they are not one and the same person, that is certainly the intended impression, and that the Gospel stands in an 'apostolic tradition' of eye-witness accounts of what Jesus said and did. Moreover, this is the only Gospel that actually tells us of the calling of Matthew, and an unpopular figure like a Jewish tax collector who becomes such a follower would be ready to draw attention in his Gospel to such an unexpected background for a follower of Christ.

For it is a very *Jewish* Gospel. Matthew's opening genealogy traces Jesus' descent back to Abraham, the 'first' devout Jew (Matt. 1:1). Joseph acts as the pious Jewish father in the infancy narrative (Matt. 1:18–25). All through Matthew's Gospel there is the tendency to try to fulfil Old Testament prophecy, starting with the prophecy that a virgin shall conceive (Isa. 7:14). Matthew clearly relies for much of his material on Mark's Gospel, as we have already seen, for example, over the narrative of the Transfiguration of Christ (see 6 August). But he interprets more teaching by Jesus, the most significant of all being the Sermon on the Mount (Matt. 5:1ff.), where Jesus appears as part new Moses and part new rabbi. Among other special characteristics are Christ's commission to Peter (Matt. 16:12–20), where the Gospel writer is concerned about the nature of the community – the *ecclesia*, or church – which is to replace the old Israel (Matt. 16:18; cf. 18:17).

Just as traditional Jewish piety was fed by the use of narrative in religious instruction, so Matthew's Gospel lends itself in a particular way to public reading. This may explain a discernible preference for using Matthew more than the other Gospel writers in the formation of the early Christian lectionaries. This Gospel appears more frequently than others in those schemes, for example on the Feast of the Transfiguration (see 6 August), and on Palm Sunday, when the Matthew passion narrative tended to be read. Matthew's account here has some special dramatic touches: he adds the story of Judas' remorse and death (Matt. 27:3–10), the message from Pilate's wife and Pilate's subsequent washing of his hands (Matt. 27:19–24), and the cosmic portents which occur immediately after Jesus' death (Matt. 27:51–3). He whose birth was signalled by a star in the East (Matt. 2:1ff.) dies a death which not only causes the curtain in the Temple to be torn, but an earthquake and the opening of tombs. The *presence* of Christ starts and ends this Gospel: '. . . and his name shall be called Emmanuel, which means, God with us' (Matt. 1:23) is how the story begins, and it concludes with the telling words, 'and lo, I am with you always, to the close of the age' (Matt. 28:20).

Matthew had to enter the calendar sooner or later. In the fifth century, a basilica was dedicated to him at Rome. But today's celebration does not appear in the West until the eighth century in the Sacramentaries that were compiled in what is now France and Germany, from where his fame spread. (He is kept in the East on 16 November.) In iconography, whereas Mark is associated with the lion (see 25 April), Matthew is identified among the four living creatures (Rev. 4:6ff.) with the face of a *man*. This may reflect the opening genealogy, where Christ's descent through Joseph is traced back to *Abraham*, the 'first' historic

Jew (Matt. 1:1), whereas Luke (the only other Gospel with a genealogy) traces his descent back to *Adam*, the archetypal human being (Luke 3:38).

Today's Collect is a revised version of that in *The Alternative Service Book (1980)* which is an adaptation of the Prayer Book Collect, with its stress on forsaking 'the selfish pursuit of gain ... that we may follow in the way of your Son Jesus Christ'. The Old Testament lesson recalls the virtues of wisdom, appropriate for a Gospel so strong on Christ the teacher (Prov. 3:13–18). The epistle, which was chosen for today in the first Prayer Books, but not in use in the Middle Ages, is the beginning of Paul's passage about the ministry committed to us, that we preach not ourselves but Jesus Christ as Lord (2 Cor. 4:1–6). The verses which follow, about 'this treasure in earthen vessels', form the epistle reading for St James the Apostle (see 25 July). The gospel passage, as we have already noted, is the calling of Matthew (Matt. 9:9–13); and the Post-Communion Prayers are the alternatives we have already met on the feasts of apostles and evangelists, either boldness to preach the gospel or the apostles' teaching and fellowship.

There is a well-known passage in the Sermon on the Mount which begins, 'You are the light of the world.' And this same theme ends today's epistle: 'For it is the God who said, "Let light shine out of darkness," [Gen. 1:3] who has shone in our hearts to give the light of the knowledge of the glory of God in the face of Christ' (2 Cor. 4:6). It is with sentiments such as these that Alec Vidler (1899–1991) ended one of his published sermons on 'The Word of God':

> The word of God calls men out of darkness into light, and out of bondage into liberty. It meets men who have the courage to doubt, and triumphs over their despair. It encourages the faint-hearted and enlarges the outlook of the narrow minded. The Bible draws men out of isolation into fellowship, for the God who speaks here is the God of your neighbour as well as of yourself, the God of the chapel as well of the church,

the God who will to draw all men together by drawing them to his Christ. The Bible can do all this for you and more, because it brings you to the place where you can hear God speaking to you personally and powerfully and where you can prove for yourself that 'God's word to us is something live, full of energy (Heb. 4:12).'

Alec Vidler, *Windsor Sermons* (London: SCM Press 1958), p. 39.

Michael and All Angels

29 September (Festival – White)

One day my mother came home enthusiastically with two gramophone records of Brahms' Requiem. On each cover sleeve was the same illustration, of Michael the Archangel weighing souls. He stood as a powerful figure, dressed in a long white flowing alb, with a red stole worn deaconwise across his chest and over the left shoulder, and over that a red cope. Two large wings somehow made their appearance through the cope at the back. All this indicated an ecclesiastical and heavenly presence. The scales he was holding were poignant. On one side was a soul going to heaven, poised in prayerful joy, whereas on the other side was a soul fearful of the torment to come as it went downwards.

Whatever people may or may not believe about life after death, there is much more half-articulated and fearful folk religion under the surface of many people's lives than is ever publicly expressed. In the later Middle Ages, many of our churches had masses repeatedly offered for the dead, so that they could be delivered from the everlasting torments of hell. Much of the horrendous mythology of the Last Judgement lives on today under the surface, and it finds expression in music, whether in the liturgical settings of the mass as in Fauré's Requiem, or in the selection of biblical material and poetry that provided the libretto for Brahms' non-liturgical Requiem.

When we look at Michael the Archangel's appearances in the Bible, it is not hard to see why his role became so developed. In the second part of the Book of Daniel, he is the helper of the chosen people (Dan. 10:13f.; 12:1). In the New Testament, he disputes with the devil (Jude 5:9), and in the Book of Revelation, he fights and slays the dragon (Rev. 12:7–9). Michael is seen as prince of hosts and a fighter.

But the Bible also has two other prominent named angels. The angel Gabriel takes the Annunciation message to Mary (Luke 1:26ff.). Raphael emerges from the Book of Tobit as a healer (Tobit 3:17). These roles are slightly adjusted in the ninth-century hymn, 'Christe sanctorum decus angelorum', where Michael is the peacemaker who banishes strife and hatred; Gabriel is the herald of heaven who helps us to spurn evil; and Raphael is the restorer, who brings strength and healing. (This hymn was translated by Athelstan Riley as 'Christ, whose fair glory of the holy angels' (*New English Hymnal*, no. 190).

Angels in general held – and still hold – a great fascination as messengers of God's will and vehicles of his presence. Angels communicate the presence of God, or give a message from God, or fight for God's purposes. In Eastern iconography, their hands are always veiled at sacred scenes, whereas humans' are not. The angels worship God in heaven but they cannot worship in the same way as humans, who have minds that often struggle to discern God's will. Angels, therefore, whether named or not, are ways of showing the personal presence of God in the world where his truth has always more to be apprehended by us. And that is why angelic protection became a popular theme in medieval prayers, for example at marriage as well as at death. At those very points when we are tempted to forget God, and to become too self-reliant, angels can break into our perceptions as sudden and unexpected incursions of God's healing and reconciliation and love. Angels, in fact, show us how our faith can be a struggle.

Michael himself was very popular in the Middle Ages. In an ancient Roman book of prayers called the Leonine Sacramentary, there are no fewer than *five* sets of mass prayers for use today. To celebrate Michael on 29 September is first known in Rome in the seventh century, probably replacing an older and more general commemoration of angels. His popular cult caused such extraordinary buildings as Mont St Michel off the coast of Brittany, and – as if to answer it on a smaller scale – St Michael's Mount off the coast of Cornwall. Cult and calendar walked hand in hand. Michael held sway on 29 September, whereas Gabriel was feasted on 24 March and Raphael on 24 November; and the 'Guardian Angels' on 2 October.

At the Reformation, the Prayer Book brought all these together under the blanket title 'Michael and All Angels'. This is, in fact, suggested by the traditional Roman Collect for 29 September, which makes no mention of Michael at all, but refers generally to the 'order of angels', because this prayer was used on this day before it was exclusively Michael's commemoration. This is the Collect used now: angels and human beings are constituted by God, and angels protect us on earth. Rightly, the 'war in heaven' between Michael and his angels and the dragon should be read today (Rev. 12:7–12). This passage was first chosen for the Prayer Book, and suitably so in view of the feasts now joined together in Michael and all the Angels. If it is read as the second lesson, then we read of Jacob's dream with the angels ascending and descending (Gen. 28:10–17). It is interesting to note that the angels *ascend* to heaven first, before they *descend* on that ladder! If the Revelation passage is read first and there is also an epistle, then the important passage at the start of the Letter to the Hebrews which distinguishes Jesus from the angels is to be read (Heb. 1:5–14 – a lection which makes up part of one of the epistles for Christmas Day). The Prayer Book followed medieval practice in choosing as the gospel Jesus teaching the disciples about becoming like children: '. . . their angels are always beholding the face of the heavenly father' (Matt. 18:1–11). However, modern revisions opt for another and more direct reading, namely the calling of Nathanael at the start of John's Gospel. This passage ends with Jesus' prophecy that Nathanael will see the angels of God ascending and descending upon him (John 1:47–51). The Post-Communion Prayer is of ancient provenance. It begins with a suitable reference to the company of angels and the spirits made perfect (Heb. 12:22) and prays that 'as in this food of our earthly pilgrimage we have shared their fellowship, so may we come to share their joy in heaven'.

Today's festival emerges from several different strands. There is the anonymity of the angels which runs right through the Bible and the Christian devotional and artistic tradition, together with another tendency to name specific prominent angels, who therefore become 'archangels'. Then we have the popular cult of Michael himself, which gave rise to church dedications, alongside the more general desire for angelic protection in a dangerous world. At the Reformation, the Anglican Reformers focused angels on one day and in doing so probably drew on an older tradition, as witness today's Collect and its all-embracing Latin original. After the Second Vatican Council, the Roman calendar did not go quite as far as this, but it did draw together the three Archangels, Michael, Gabriel, and Raphael, to be commemorated on one single feast today. These carefully crafted prayers and readings are intended for a world that may have different priorities, but still has time and use for unconscious doors to the presence of God, which are entirely legitimate, as they feed the religious imagination, with Christ himself at the centre.

In 1827, John Keble (1792–1866) published a collection of poems for the Sundays and Holy Days of the Christian Year. It was a bestseller throughout the nineteenth century. The following two verses are the first and the last which are suggested for devotion today. In a style that is typical of the author, they kindle the imagination and suggest the personal presence of God as protector, messenger, and healer, in the traditions associated with the three Archangels:

> Ye stars that round the Sun of righteousness
>   In glorious order roll,
> With harps for ever strung, ready to bless
>   God for each rescued soul,
> Ye eagle spirits, that build in light divine,
>   Oh! think of us to-day,

Faint warblers of this earth, that would combine
    Our trembling notes with your accepted lay.

Grant, Lord, that when around th'expiring world
    Our seraph guardians wait,
While on her death-bed, ere to ruin hurl'd,
    She owns Thee, all too late,
They to their charge may turn, and thankful see
    Thy mark upon us still;
Then all together rise, and reign with Thee,
    And all their holy joy o'er contrite hearts fulfil!

John Keble, *The Christian Year*
(London & Glasgow: Blackie, n.d.), pp. 309f.

Luke the Evangelist

18 October (Festival – Red)

I once played a game with a parish house group and asked them which Gospel they would take to a desert island, if they had to make the choice. The ensuing discussion proved most revealing! Of course personalities and temperaments vary, though I am not keen on categorizing or stereotyping unduly. But what did emerge was a growing appreciation of just how different each one is. At the risk of over-simplifying, each emerges as follows: Matthew is the Jewish portrayal of Christ the teacher who fulfils Old Testament prophecies, and much else besides. Mark is the at times almost aggressively direct narrative of a Jesus who begins as an adult baptized by John and whose tomb is fled by his followers in terror, and much else besides. John, on the other hand, has far more teaching from Jesus, surrounding specific miracles, and portrays Christ's glorification on the cross.

When it comes to Luke, we are again on different ground. Luke could well have been the only Gospel writer who was not Jewish, which comes across in the language which he uses. He has a more extended sequence of infancy narratives surrounding the births of John the Baptist and of Jesus than Matthew (Luke 1:1–2:52). Luke traces Jesus' descent back to Adam, the 'first' human being, to emphasize that salvation is for all (Luke 3:38). Jesus prays at specific points in the Gospel (Luke 3:21; 5:16; 16:12; 9:18,28; 11:1), most notably for those nailing him to the cross at the crucifixion (Luke 23:34). He is more concerned than any other Gospel writer with women, hence the prominent position of Mary before the birth of Christ (Luke 1:26ff.); Jesus' compassion for the widow of Nain when he raises her son from the dead (Luke 7:11–17); the number of women who followed him and their service to him (Luke 8:1–3); and his address to the daughters of Jerusalem on his way to the cross (Luke 23:27f.) Luke is also concerned about Jesus' seeking and saving the lost, hence the parables of the lost sheep, the lost coin and the prodigal son (Luke 15:1–32).

We have already observed the power and influence of the infancy narratives, as they give rise to such feasts as the Presentation in the Temple (2 February) and the Annunciation (25 March), as well as the Nativity of John the Baptist (24 June). Luke's narrative of the passion, however, has several special characteristics. Jesus is tried and condemned by the Sanhedrin at dawn and not by night; Pontius Pilate insists on Christ's innocence, asserting this no fewer than three times; and there is – unlike in the other Gospel writers – a trial before Herod (Luke 23:1–25). Jesus is innocent, just as Luke portrays Stephen (Acts 7), and Jesus dies in faithful trust, commending himself to the Father (Luke 23:46); this can be compared to the way Stephen prays to Jesus at his death, 'Lord Jesus, receive my spirit' (Acts 7:59). Jesus' ministry of healing and compassion is apparent, as he heals the servant of the High Priest who was wounded by Peter's sword (Luke 22:51). He looks on Peter after he had publicly denied him (Luke 22:61), and he pardons the penitent thief (Luke 23:39–43).

Luke's style is idiomatic and elegant Greek and there are occasions when one can sense, even in translation, a deliberate smoothing of material that he uses from Mark (Luke 4:31–7; cf. Mark 1:21–8). Although he was not one of the apostles, some have identified him, as in the case of Matthias and Mark, as one of the seventy commissioned by Jesus himself (Luke 10:1f.); this is the passage that has tended to be read today as the gospel. He was clearly a significant figure in the early Church, as he wrote both a Gospel and an account of the unfolding life of that Church, the Acts of the Apostles. He was a companion of Paul on the missionary journeys (Acts 16:10f.,25f., 27–8). As a physician (Col. 4:14) he is the patron saint of doctors, but artists have also looked to him. He has been portrayed as the ox among the four living creatures (Rev. 4:6f.), which has sometimes been interpreted to reflect the patient beast of burden, though it also fits in with the sacrificial imagery of the Temple, where his Gospel both starts and ends, in the praise of God. In this connection, Luke – uniquely – provides us with three liturgical hymns in full, the Magnificat (Luke 1:46–55), the Benedictus (Luke 1:68–79) and the Nunc Dimittis (Luke 2:29–32); and he also gives us, with the beginning of the song of the angels, the Gloria in Excelsis (Luke 2:14). Like a skilled writer, he tells us almost nothing about himself directly in either the Gospel or the Acts of the Apostles. Surprisingly, it was not until the ninth century that he is commemorated today, among those Sacramentaries compiled in what is now France and Germany. They probably took the idea from the East, where he is also commemorated on this day, an agreement which is another sign of his universal significance.

Today's Collect is a revision of that which is contained in *The Alternative Service Book (1980)*, but with the addition of significant phrases from the Prayer Book Collect ('whose praise is in the gospel' and 'the wholesome medicine of the gospel'). For the first reading, there is a choice. Isaiah's call to 'strengthen the weak hands' and his prophecy that 'the eyes of the blind may be opened' (Isa. 35:3–6) are appropriate for the physician-evangelist and his narrative of Christ the healer. Alternatively there is the account of the beginning of the second missionary journey undertaken by Luke and Paul (Acts 16:6–12a). This latter passage has its own internal drama in that towards the end we encounter the first of the three 'we' sections (Acts 16:10–17; 16:25–21:18; 27:1–28:16). These have been much discussed by scholars but it is now generally agreed that they are editorial signs of an earlier draft of these events, when Luke and Paul were together. The epistle reading is the exhortation to endure suffering, part of which is read when Peter and Paul are commemorated (see 29 June); but it is chosen here also because Luke is mentioned by name (2 Tim. 4:5–17). The gospel, as we have noted, is the mission of the seventy (Luke 10:1–9) and the Post-Communion Prayer once more uses *The Alternative Service Book (1980)* Pentecost Collect, or a prayer from the Canadian *Book of Alternative Services* (1985).

Luke's portrait of Christ, is, as we have seen, one that draws salvation for the lost. Luke is unique in giving us that sequence of the lost sheep, the lost coin and the prodigal son (Luke 15:1–32). These have inspired artists and preachers across the centuries. In Christina Rossetti's poem, 'A Prodigal Son', are some reflections on this parable:

> Does that lamp still burn in my Father's house,
>   Which he kindled the night I went away?
> I turned once beneath the cedar boughs,
>   And marked it gleam with a golden ray;
>   Did he think to light me home some day?

The Works of Christina Rossetti, with an introduction
by Martin Corner, and bibliography (Wordsworth Poetry
Library) (Ware: Wordsworth, 1995), pp. 378f.

Simon and Jude, Apostles

28 October (Festival – Red)

Who were the apostles Simon and Jude? Simon appears in the lists of the Apostles. He is referred to as 'Simon the Canaanite' (but this word may mean 'enthusiast') in the first two Gospels (Matt. 10:4; Mark 3:18), whereas in the other two, he is called 'Simon the Zealot' (Luke 6:15; Acts 1:13). Simon is often portrayed with a fish. Jude, on the other hand, is referred to as Judas son of James in the two Lucan versions (Luke 6:16; Acts 1:13) and he is often identified as the 'Thaddeus' in the other two versions (Matt. 10:3; Mark 3:18). He also receives a solitary honorable mention in the Fourth Gospel, where he is described as Judas 'not Iscariot', and he asks Jesus, 'Lord, how is it that you will manifest yourself to us, and not to the world?' (John 14:22). Thus he asks the sharp question that is on everyone's lips. A short epistle bearing his name is to be found between the third epistle of John and the Book of Revelation at the end of the New Testament. He is often regarded as the patron saint of hopeless cases, because no-one invoked him for anything since so little is known about him! According to one tradition, Simon and Jude were supposed to have preached the gospel and met their martyrs' death in Persia. Jude is supposed to have been clubbed to death – hence his occasional portrayal with a club.

They are celebrated separately in the East, where Simon occurs on 10 May, and Jude on 19 June. But in the West they have always been commemorated together, like Philip and James (see 2 May), and we first come across them at the end of the eighth century in the Sacramentaries that were written in what is now France and Germany. Thereafter they appear at Rome in the tenth century. Being so obviously scriptural, they were retained at the Reformation in the Prayer Books on their feast day. Today's Collect is that of *The Alternative Service Book (1980)*. It is based directly on the Prayer Book, with its echoes of the letter to the Ephesians – being founded on the apostles and prophets and joined together in the unity of the Spirit (Eph. 2:20–3; 4:3). The foundation stone continues in the first reading, 'Behold I am laying an ensign for a foundation stone, a tested stone' (Isa. 28:14–16). The epistle is the same passage which inspired the first part of the Collect, the foundation of the Church (Eph. 2:19–22). This provision is new, since the Prayer Book directs the reading of the first part of the letter of Jude (Jude 1:1–9), which ends on the theme of judgement. The gospel carries on from the 'farewell discourse' in the reading for St Barnabas (see 11 June) with the call of Jesus that the disciples should love one another (John 15:17–27). The Post-Communion Prayer provision, once again, consists of those two alternative prayers, from Pentecost in *The Alternative Service Book (1980)* and the Canadian *Book of Alternative Services* (1985).

These two anonymous saints have inspired a more anonymous and therefore general reflection on the nature of Christian discipleship. One of the great commentaries on the Apostles' Creed was written in the seventeenth century by John Pearson (1613–86), who has this to say on the communion of saints:

> Because there is more than an outward vocation, and a charitable presumption, necessary to make a man holy; therefore we must find some other qualification which must make him really and truly such, not only by an extrinsical denomination, but by a real and internal affection. What this sanctity is, and who are capable of this title properly, we must learn out of the gospel of Christ; by which alone, ever since the Church of Christ was founded, any man can become a saint.

John Pearson, *An Exposition of the Creed*, ed. James Nichols (London: Ward Lock, 1854), p. 504.

All Saints' Day

1 November (Principal Feast – White or Gold)

There is a sense of completion and yet open-endedness about today's feast. How can it be possible for the 'all' of this day to say what it means? How can the number of the holy ones of God ever reach completion this side of heaven?

This is the message that comes across from a reading of history, from a reflection upon the human predicament, and also from the pages of the New Testament. For in the good news of Christ, we have to live with an extraordinary paradox, that the gospel engages us and identifies with us, but at the same time challenges us and makes us uncomfortable. There are some saints who have preached wonderful and eloquent sermons, and have made hearers stir in their hearts so that they felt part of the Kingdom of Heaven straight away. There have been others, however, who by their righteous indignation and passion for justice have humbled people, and have always made them feel challenged to the extent of regarding themselves as unworthy of Christ.

This is why for centuries the All Saints' Day gospel has consisted of the first twelve verses of the Sermon on the Mount (Matt. 5:1–12). Many people have leapt straight to the words of Christ, which are obviously of profound importance. But the opening words set an important context. Jesus *sees* the crowds. Then he goes up the mountain. Then he sits down like a teacher ready to address his followers. Only at that stage do they come to him to listen. Each one of those actions is significant. They imply a relationship that is already present between Christ and his disciples before he even opens his mouth. They already know something about him and are therefore ready to hear more. He already knows them, and his body language is one of acceptance and preparedness – he sees, he goes up, he sits down to wait for them. Often we expect the reverse, if not of Christ, then of ourselves. We have to rush in with Jesus and force-feed others with our version of his words. Prior relationships, preparing the ground, looking at and accepting other people – these are ways of making ready for Christ to speak.

And how does this sermon begin? It begins by identifying a series of reversals. The poor in spirit – not the rich – are to have the Kingdom of Heaven. Those who mourn – not those who are crying out for attention – are going to be comforted. The meek – not the grabbing consumers – will inherit the earth. Those who hunger and thirst for righteousness are going to be satisfied – the very people who appear never to stop bothering us with the truth. The merciful will obtain mercy – because they themselves know best what mercy really means. The pure in heart will see God – because they are single-hearted, and intent in their search for the truth. The peacemakers are those who will be the children of God – because by their relentless belief that peace is possible, they catch a glimpse of their heavenly Father. Those who are per-secuted for righteousness' sake – not those who know easy success – will have the Kingdom of Heaven. And those who are reviled are indeed blessed – because that is how things have always been, as the prophets before Christ knew all too well.

Here is one of the most complete and yet open-ended expressions of the Christian gospel. Here is a passage that can be read on All Saints' Day, because these words both put everything together and at the same time leave enough unsaid. This may explain why All Saints is celebrated in the East on the first Sunday after Pentecost (they know nothing of Trinity Sunday). For it is only after working through Advent, Christmas and Epiphany, Lent, Holy Week and Easter, Ascension and Pentecost that the full impact of the gospel can be felt and celebrated. In the Coptic and Ethiopian Churches, 4 November has long been kept as a celebration of the four living creatures, the lion, the ox, the man and the eagle (Rev. 4:6f.). An old Jewish commentator, writing on those beasts as they are described in Ezekiel 1:10, describes them as follows: 'Man is exalted among creatures, the eagle among birds, the ox among domestic animals, the lion among wild beasts; all of them have received dominion . . . yet they are stationed below the chariot of the Holy One.' Perhaps this quaint commemoration is its own reminder that it is not only glorified humans who sing God's praises for ever, but the whole new creation as well.

When did the feast of All Saints first appear on this day? The answer is not entirely straightforward. It appears that Rome originally followed the Eastern practice and kept All Saints on the Sunday after Pentecost. Then on the anniversary of the consecration of the Pantheon to Christian usage by Pope Boniface IV, in 609 or 610, All Saints was celebrated on 13 May. It was not until the time of Pope Gregory III (731–41) that a chapel to 'All the Saints' was dedicated in St Peter's Basilica on 1 November. In the following century it was declared a feast throughout the Western Church and it is found in northern Europe increasingly from that time onwards. Christian iconography for All Saints' Day in the old manuscript service books is occasionally lavish in depicting the Adoration of the Lamb surrounded by those four living creatures; and many a cross has been crafted since that time with the same pattern, namely the lamb in the centre and the four beasts at the four points. Here is the lamb of sacrifice, on the throne, and the four living creatures symbolizing the creation made new, the four evangelists, and all who have been addressed in one way or another by them as part of that eternal work.

At the English Reformation, the number of saints in the calendar was drastically reduced, so that All Saints' Day stood out with a prominence that it never had before. Sometimes pruning can help to clarify where priorities are. The Reformation deliberately played down and then excluded the traditional piety of the preceding centuries which divided those who have died into the saints, who can pray for us, and who are commemorated today, and the departed, for whom we on earth must pray, on All Souls' Day, tomorrow. This division only came about in time as the second feast gained in popularity, from its inception in the ninth century.

But the Church needs to take care in defining too closely these categories, and more ancient forms of prayer which are still known in the East would find such an approach arbitrary. An early eucharistic prayer, probably written by the great fourth-century teacher Basil of Caesarea, approaches this area with some welcome reticence: 'Since, Master, it is a command of your only begotten Son that we should share in the commemoration of your saints, vouchsafe to remember, Lord, those of our Fathers who have been pleasing to you from eternity: patriarchs, prophets, apostles, martyrs, confessors, preachers, evangelists, and all the righteous perfected in faith . . .' And it goes on to ask for the prayers of Mary, in the context of the work of Christ, and not in her own right.

There are some differences of emphasis here. Some people will welcome the categorization implicit in All Saints' and All Souls' Days. Others may see in them differences of *context*; we can rejoice in the lives, examples, and fellowship of the saints today, and mourn specific loved ones tomorrow – but in the same basic Christian hope.

Such reticence may well have inspired today's Collect, which goes back to the Prayer Book, with its eloquent reference to 'the inexpressible joys that you have prepared for those who truly love you'. The two classic readings are the vision of the angel appearing and the number of those sealed in the twelve tribes of Israel (Rev. 7:9–17) and the first part of the Sermon on the Mount (Matt. 5:1–12). The epistle reading anchors these two passages in the simple truth that we are God's children (1 John 3:1–3). The new lection scheme follows *The Promise of His Glory* (1991) in providing for a three-year cycle of readings, which brings All Saints' Day into line with Sundays. This is intended as an enrichment to the readings just described, for Year A. In Year B there is a choice between the souls of the righteous in the hand of God (Wisd. 3:1–9) and the rich feast on the mountain at the end of time (Isa. 25:6–9). For the epistle, there is the new heaven and the new earth (Rev. 21:1–6a), and for the gospel, the raising of Lazarus (John 11:32–44). (Year B concentrates on Mark's Gospel, and also uses appropriate material from the Fourth Gospel, hence the Lazarus narrative.) For Year C, there is Daniel's vision (Dan. 7:1–3, 15–18), for the epistle, the riches of the inheritance of the saints (Eph. 1:11–23), and the gospel consists of the opening verses of Luke's 'Sermon' – this time on the plain, not on the mount (Luke 6:20–31); this is, again, an appropriate choice, given that in Year C, Luke's Gospel has priority. The Post-Communion Prayer looks on the eucharistic feeding of 'strangers and pilgrims here on earth' (cf. Heb. 11:13) in the hope of a welcome 'with all your Saints to the heavenly feast on the day of your Kingdom'. This is a new composition, in *The Promise of His Glory* (1991), and inspired by All Saints' Day prayers from recent centuries.

The saints do not belong to any religious tradition. In the seventeenth century, Richard Baxter (1615–91) was among those who protested at the formality of Anglican order and worship to the extent that he left the Church of England at the Restoration. In 1681, his *Poetical Fragments* were published. These contain the following verses in a long hymn 'written when I was silenced and cast out'. As in the Beatitudes themselves, we sometimes have to reach depths to discover the full measure of God's love and mercy.

> He wants not friends that hath thy love,
>   And may converse and walk with thee,
> And with thy saints here and above,
>   With whom for ever I must be . . .
>
> As for my friends, they are not lost;
>   The several vessels of thy fleet,
> Though parted now, by tempests tost,
>   Shall safely in thy haven meet . . .

The heavenly hosts, world without end,
    Shall be my company above;
And thou, my best and surest Friend,
    Who shall divide me from thy love?

Maurice Frost (ed.), *Historical Companion to Hymns Ancient and Modern* (London: Clowes, 1962), no. 274, verses 1, 3, 6.

Andrew the Apostle, Patron of Scotland

30 November (Festival – Red)

I have known the St Andrew's cross all my life. The white 'saltire' cross against the pale blue background is a flag that Scots have known for centuries. Quite why Andrew is associated with Scotland is explained by a legend that St Rule brought his relics from Patras in Greece, where he is said to have been crucified on a saltire cross, to Scotland. He is supposed to have halted at a place in Fife which now bears the Saint's name, and built a church there. Whatever the exact truth behind this story, it is hard to avoid the conclusion that to name a town St Andrews rests on ancient tradition, however reliable it may be.

But who was St Andrew? He was the brother of Simon Peter and therefore one of the first to be called by Christ (Matt. 4:18; Mark 1:16), and he appears in the lists of the Apostles (Matt. 10:2; Mark 3:18; Luke 6:21; Acts 1:13). Mark also has Andrew and Simon hosting Jesus when he left the synagogue at Capernaum (Mark 1:29); and Peter, James, and Andrew are the ones who ask Jesus on the Mount of Olives, 'Tell us, when will this be, and what will be the sign when these things are all to be accomplished?' (Mark 13:3).

Once again, however, the Fourth Gospel gives us the most nuanced account. Andrew is the first who hears of Christ, and he goes to his brother Simon Peter with the words, 'We have found the Messiah' (John 1:40). He and his brother, like Philip, are from Bethsaida (John 1:44). Before the feeding of the five thousand, when Philip has declared that 200 denarii would not buy enough bread to feed the multitude, it is Andrew who says, 'There is a lad here who has five barley loaves and two fish; but what are they among so many?' (John 6:8). When the Greeks appear at the Passover Festival, Philip and Andrew go to Jesus and inform him that these visitors have asked, 'Sir, we wish to see Jesus' (John 12:22).

What emerges from this portrait? He is quick on the scene and ahead of even Simon Peter, when Jesus is around. He is quick to point out to Jesus even the minimal resources available to feed the five thousand. He is quick to point out to Jesus that there are foreign visitors who want to see him. It is not hard to conclude that the Andrew depicted in these scenes is a person intended to come across as someone who takes initiatives.

Although he is the brother of Simon Peter, he never becomes part of that 'inner cabinet' of Peter, and the two brothers James and John, who in the other three Gospels accompanied Jesus, for example, up the mountain for the Transfiguration (Matt. 17:1–9; Mark 9:1–9; Luke 9:28–36). Andrew thus has somewhat different characteristics in the Fourth Gospel from those given in the other three accounts.

As the brother of Peter, however, he enters the calendar early. He has been commemorated today in Jerusalem from the beginning of the fifth century, and in Rome during the time of Pope Simplicius (468–83). However, the gospel passage in the East is the version of the call of Andrew from the Fourth Gospel (John 1:35–44), where he precedes Peter, and he is referred to in the calendars of the Byzantine rite as the 'first-called'. But in the West, with its traditional concentration on Peter, the gospel has always been Matthew's account, in which they are called at the same time (Matt. 4:18–22). At the turn of the fifth and sixth centuries, a church was dedicated to St Andrew below St Peter's in Rome, as if to express subordination. Churches were dedicated to him in Italy, France, and in Anglo-Saxon England.

Today's Collect is a revision of that in *The Alternative Service Book (1980)*, with echoes from that composed for the Prayer Book. It alludes to Andrew bringing his brother Peter to Christ, following the Fourth Gospel account. The reference to the 'good news of your kingdom' may reflect the fact that the season of Advent has either just begun or is just about to. The Old Testament reading is about the messenger announcing peace (Isa. 52:7–10), again suitable at Advent. The epistle, like the Old Testament reading, stresses the preaching of the good news, another suggestion of Advent (Rom. 10:12–18); it is the same passage substantially as was read in the Middle Ages and in the Prayer Book, though the latter is somewhat longer. The gospel appropriately narrates the calling of Simon Peter and Andrew his brother, casting their nets as fishermen (Matt. 4:18–22), the same passage that has been read on this day in the West for centuries. But since the Collect follows the Fourth Gospel version of Andrew's call, it would have been more congruous to have chosen that passage instead (John 1:35–44), as in the East. The Post-Communion Prayer is the same provision made on the other feasts of apostles and evangelists, namely the second Collect in *The Alternative Service Book (1980)* for Pentecost, or the prayer from the Canadian *Book of Alternative Services* (1985).

There is a sense of mobility and cost that emerges from today's feast. The proclamation of the good news of the coming of the Kingdom rings through as Advent seeps into the Church's worship. That calling of the first two fishermen by the lakeside, as the gospel reading indicates, tells us what is at stake when Jesus beckons us to him. In a famous sermon preached by C. S. Lewis (1898–1963) in the shadow of the start of the Second World War, entitled 'The Christian in Danger', the claims of Christ ring out in all their awesome challenge:

It is for a very different reason that religion cannot occupy the whole of life in the sense of excluding all our natural activities. For, of course, in some sense, it must occupy the whole of life. There is no question of a compromise between the claims of God and the claims of culture, or politics, or anything else. God's claim is infinite and inexorable. You can refuse it; or you can begin to try to grant it. There is no middle way.

Ashley Sampson (ed.), *Famous English Sermons* (London: Religious Book Club, 1942), p. 372.

Christmas Day

25 December (Principal Feast – White or Gold)

For my thirteenth birthday I was given a book of large colour photographs of paintings from the eleventh to the fifteenth centuries depicting the life of Christ. When I opened the parcel it was not really a surprise, as I had seen the book in a shop in Edinburgh on a visit there with my parents and they obviously observed my glee as I took it out of its case and thumbed through the pages. For the Nativity of Christ, a rich painting by Barna Da Siena (who died in 1351) was chosen. It is a characteristically rich ensemble. The baby Jesus lies in the centre against a gold background. Mary, dressed in deep blue, and with her halo the same colour of gold as the large halo surrounding Jesus, kneels in prayer and amazement. To the right, Joseph slumbers in relief. He is much older than Mary, but unlike her is dressed in rich gold, like his halo. Up in the top right-hand corner, two shepherds gaze into the light in the sky, as does one of their sheep, suggesting their eventual arrival on the scene.

So far, everything is faithful to the narrative in Luke's Gospel (Luke 2:1–20). But there are additions as well, suggested by legends and traditions that grew up after the time of the New Testament. The ox and the ass represent nature's recognition of the arrival of the Saviour, suggested by Isaiah's prophecy that 'the ox knows his master, and the ass his master's crib; but Israel does not know, and my people does not understand' (Isa. 1:3). Two midwives are depicted on the far left, called Zelemi and Salome, one looking away, the other looking on. And the whole scene takes place in a *cave*, which was apparently identified at an early stage, and where Christians went to venerate.

Caves are frequent in that part of Judea. Here once more we see an example of the need to state the particularity of the gospel, centring on a particular person born at a particular time, and in a particular place.

The painting is a mixture of Luke's narrative and popular legend. And that is how the Christmas story is often told. Here is a baby born in natural surroundings, and in unexpected circumstances. He is surrounded by the human race, responding as best they can; a young mother who finds herself pregnant, still full of faith and devotion; an aged father who is blessed by God, and who has carried out his task with faithfulness; two midwives who have helped the young mother through the potentially fraught experience of the birth of the first child; and two shepherds, on their way to pay their visit. The whole scene mixes the ordinary and the extraordinary, and – like the incarnation itself – it is both an overwhelmingly single event, focused on Jesus in the golden centre, and an experience made up of small fragments of human response in the periphery.

We do not know when the Nativity of Christ first appeared in the calendar, but we do know for certain that it was observed in Rome in the year 336 on this day. In the pagan Roman calendar, this was the day when the birth of the 'Unconquered son' was celebrated, which had been instituted at Rome by the Emperor Aurelian in 274. No doubt early Christians interpreted the prophecy of Malachi that 'the sun of righteousness shall rise, with healing in its wings' (Mal. 4:2) as a manifestation of the One True God. Alternatively, as we noted in our discussion of Epiphany (see 6 January), according to an old tradition, the Lord was crucified on the same day of the year as the Annunciation, and since this was on 25 March, his birth would be nine months later. Whichever of these theories is the correct one, the fact remains that 25 December spread throughout the East and West as the day on which the birth of Christ was observed, and East and West kept both 25 December and 6 January as celebrations of the Nativity and the Epiphany respectively, and with differing emphases; only the Armenian Church has one feast, on 6 January, and of the birth of Christ only – we cannot all be the same!

Art, literature and popular devotion have tended to place even greater emphasis on Christmas than on Easter. The overall shape of the liturgical year serves to encourage this tendency, as we travel through Advent to Christmas as the first festival, and then through Lent towards Holy Week on to Easter, and thereafter into Ascension and Pentecost. These two 'cycles' are intended to complement one another, enabling us to see a foreshadowing of suffering around the crib scene, which is sharpened by the commemoration of the Holy Innocents (see 28 December).

It has long been appropriate to celebrate more than one Eucharist at Christmas and Easter, as ancient practice in the East and West and contemporary custom demonstrate. In the old Roman lectionaries, which were eventually used in one form or another throughout the West, there are three masses for Christmas. Up to the fifth century, however, there was only one Eucharist, whose readings were those which appear in the Prayer Book, namely the opening of the letter to the Hebrews, with its string of quotations from the Old Testament to demonstrate Christ's supremacy over the angels and the redemption wrought by him (Heb. 1:1–12), and the enigmatic prologue to the Fourth Gospel (John 1:1–14). It sometimes seems strange to Christmas worshippers that two such unpictorial lessons should have been read on this day for so many centuries. Nowadays, it is common to shorten the Hebrews reading so that it ends just before the Old Testament quotations, having stated its basic message (Heb. 1:1–4). On the other hand, the Prologue to John's Gospel is frequently introduced at Christmas Carol Services with the words, 'St John unfolds the great mystery of the Incarnation', when in fact for many people he is not unfolding it, but making it yet more mysterious! John's Gospel does not narrate the birth of Christ as an historic event, like Matthew (Matt. 1:1–25) and Luke (Luke 2:1–7). The Prologue is more of an introduction to a religious drama. It sets the Incarnation of the Word made flesh in a cosmic context, and the expression, 'and we beheld his glory' (John 1:14), refers to the glory of Christ in its entirety, which for John is focused on the cross. At Christmas, however, this 'glory' takes more worshippers to the crib of popular piety than to the crucifixion.

The second Eucharist of Christmas appeared in Rome when Pope Xystus III (435–40) rebuilt an old pagan building and had it dedicated to the Virgin Mary. It is commonly called Santa Maria Maggiore, and it was there that the Eucharist was celebrated at *night*, not necessarily at midnight. (The morning mass was celebrated in St Peter's.) Its epistle is the grace of God 'appearing' (the same word as 'Epiphany') for the salvation of all (Titus 2:11–15), and the gospel is Luke's narrative of the birth of Christ and the arrival of the shepherds (Luke 1:1–14).

The third Eucharist was added in the sixth century, and celebrated at dawn in the church of St Anastasius as it was conveniently situated near the residence of the Byzantine Governor at the time. Its readings are the appearance of the Saviour 'by the washing of regeneration' (Titus 3:4–7) and the departure of the shepherds from Bethlehem to go out and proclaim the Saviour's birth (Luke 2:15–20).

These three sets of readings provide a kind of sequence. The *night* Eucharist tells of the birth of Christ and the arrival of the shepherds. The *dawn* Eucharist narrates their departure – an often neglected scene. And the *day* Eucharist, with its lengthy epistle, provides a more obviously theological framework. Many people nowadays choose to vary these readings, and there is an argument to suggest that the prologue to John is more appropriate at midnight, with the surrounding darkness, in which the light shines, and the more pictorial narratives fit better on Christmas morning.

The recent revisions have added Old Testament lessons, all from Isaiah. These are the prophecy that a virgin shall conceive (Isa. 9:2–7); the watchman who will wait all day and night, and the coming salvation of God (Isa. 62:6–12); and the herald who brings good tidings (Isa. 52:7–10), which is also appointed for St Andrew's Day (see 30 November). The first Prayer Book

(1549) retained the night and the day Eucharists only, with their readings, but in 1552 these were reduced further to one provision only, with the epistle and gospel for the day Eucharist, namely the opening words of Hebrews (Heb. 1:1–14) and the prologue to John (John 1:1–14). Anglican practice has recovered the 1549 pattern over the past century, to great advantage.

The present provision offers three sets of readings, which are, at root, those of the three traditional Christmas Eucharists of the ancient West, to which have been added three Old Testament readings. These can be used as and when appropriate. The prayers provided for today, however, presuppose not three Eucharists but two, namely one at night and one on Christmas morning. The Collect for Christmas Night is taken from *The Alternative Service Book (1980)*, and *The Promise of His Glory* (1991), and is a reworking of the old Roman Collect for this occasion, with its allusions to the atmosphere of the service, 'who made this most holy night to shine with the brightness of your One True Light'. The Post-Communion Prayer is from *The Promise of His Glory* (1991), and yet more directly places the worshipper before the altar in the middle of the night, looking forward to the time when 'the day dawns and Christ the morning star rises in our hearts'.

The Collect for Christmas Day, however, is taken from the Prayer Book, which carefully combines three significant truths about the Incarnation: the only begotten Son takes our nature upon him; and this means that we are both born again by adoption and grace, and are daily renewed by the Holy Spirit. In other words, there is an *annual* commemoration of the birth of Christ, and a *daily* renewal as adopted children. Here we have a gentle hint that Christmas is not an annual truth but a daily reality. Today's Post-Communion Prayer comes from the Canadian *Book of Alternative Services* (1985), which prays that the light of faith may illuminate our hearts. The opening reference to 'whose word has come among us in the Holy Child of Bethlehem' neatly draws together the John prologue (John 1:1–14) and the birth of Christ (Luke 2:1–7).

George Herbert (1593–1633) was probably one of the greatest poets of his generation. In 1633 *The Temple* was published, just after his death. His poetry is succinct and powerful, with its direct combination of imagery. In the following words, which come from the poem entitled 'Christmas', Herbert subtly combines the truths of the Christmas readings and the Prayer Book Collect – which as a priest he would have known well – and prays for the work of redemption in the worshipper:

> O Thou, whose glorious, yet contracted light,
>   Wrapt in night's mantle, stole into a manger;
> Since my dark soul and brutish is thy right,
>   To Man of all beasts be not thou a stranger:
> Furnish and deck my soul, that thou mayst have
> A better lodging than a rack or grave.

The Poems of George Herbert, with an introduction by Arthur Waugh (London: Oxford University Press, 1955), p. 72.

Stephen, Deacon and Martyr

26 December (Festival – Red)

'Second Christmas Day' is the name given to 26 December in Denmark. I remember being told this before we spent our first Christmas with my grandparents in Aarhus in 1954. The journey there stands particularly in my memory, because the North Sea was as flat as a duckpond on the way across from Harwich, but the return trip was quite different – storm doors were put up before we even left the harbour. Nature seemed to express first and second Christmas Day in that venerable tradition: whereas on the first day the birth of Christ is celebrated, on the second it is the martyrdom of Stephen. Gold vestments and the Christmas readings are the obvious diet for one occasion, but red vestments and the martyrdom of Stephen (Acts 7:51–60) are the more austere diet for the second, more sombre occasion.

Why spoil the fun? One answer is that it is in the calendar, and the book is there to be observed. But people need more than just an explanation, they need justifying. The justifying we have already met; the Annunciation (see 25 March) almost deliberately gets in the way of the great events of Holy Week and Easter. Even when we are most intent on looking at the cross, we are still beckoned to the birth of Christ, which is strengthened by the ancient tradition which maintains that Christ was conceived and died on the same day. In the same manner, the Christmas celebration takes us from birth to death straight away, and continues to do so in the Holy Innocents of the day after (see 28 December).

Who was Stephen? He is yet one more character given directly to us by Luke, this time in the Acts of the Apostles. The first

Jerusalem Christians decided to appoint seven servants, 'deacons', to assist in the work of the Church, and to lighten the load of the apostles. The daily distribution to widows was not functioning properly and it seems that the Greek-speaking community felt neglected. Seven men were accordingly chosen, the first of whom was Stephen. They were set before the apostles, and prayer was offered with the laying on of hands (Acts 6:1–6). It would seem that it was Stephen's *actions* rather than his *words* that brought him into immediate controversy with the Jewish authorities. He was brought before the High Priest – where he made a great speech in his defence (Acts 7:1–53). This speech is an account of the good purposes of God in the old covenant and how these are fulfilled in the new. It is hard-hitting to those who refused to recognize Jesus, namely the Jewish authorities. Perhaps Luke intends us to understand that Stephen knew what was coming and that this was his last chance. At any rate, he was taken out and stoned to death. At the moment of his death, he was filled with the Spirit, and saw the glory of God and Jesus standing at his right hand; and he commended himself to Jesus (Acts 7:54–60), in words that echo Luke's account of Jesus' own death, when he commends his spirit into his Father's hands (Luke 23:46).

There are many parallels between Luke's narratives of Jesus and Stephen at their deaths. Both are innocent, both commend themselves to God in trust at the end, both pray for those who are killing them, and both die outside the city. But care is taken to draw contrasts between the two; Stephen is not crucified, he points to Jesus throughout, both in his speech and in his prayer, and whereas Jesus dies surrounded by a small band of sympathizers, Stephen dies surrounded by his accusers. He is the first Christian martyr. This is how he has been referred to in both East and West across the centuries, and it is good that this title has been restored in the recent Anglican revisions. For the early Church drew strength from the blood of the martyrs. They left deep in the corporate memory of the Christian community not discussion about pain but the experience of suffering.

In both East and West, there has been a tradition that began from the fourth and fifth centuries of placing Stephen, John and the Holy Innocents close to Jesus' birth; the first martyr, the disciple whom Jesus loved (see 27 December), and those who died innocently in the wake of Christ's birth (see 28 December). The significance of this trio of feasts cannot be overestimated, even if they are frequently neglected in practice because many people have run out of energy when Christmas Day is over! Luke takes pains to tell us that a persecution arose after the death of Stephen (Acts 11:19), and he is described as a martyr (= witness) by Paul in his speech to the people in Jerusalem (Acts 22:20).

How can this painful juxtaposition of what the Danes call first and second Christmas Day really work out? The answer is to be found in a hymn that is usually sung on this day. Hymns are an integral part of Lutheran piety, and the nineteenth-century hymn-writer Frederik Hammerich wrote a hymn that draws Stephen into the Bethlehem scene with a profoundly touching realism. Here are two stanzas translated rather literally into blank verse, in the first of which there is a play on the word 'wreath': in Greek it is *stephanos*, the meaning of Stephen's name, and a wreath is a symbol of victory:

> Hail, little child, laid in a crib,
> Prince of Christmas, yet our reconciler with God!
> To you belong all praise and might,
> The Crown of Heaven, and of all life.
> How radiates today with special splendour
> Over your crib that wreath
> With which your martyr Stephen is adorned
> Because you took him suddenly away from us!
>
> The peace of the Christmas angels comes down
> Upon the eyes of the glorified Stephen,
> And the power and glory of Christmas
> Are revealed in his death.

So he fell into a sweet heavenly sleep,
On his bed of stones, unharmed,
Like a babe in his mother's arms.

Here crib and martyrdom are brought together and they indicate that Stephen, who became a popular subject of church dedications, is indeed appropriately commemorated today. Moreover, the fact that he was a deacon, an order of ministry that is only today being properly recovered in the West, is a way of setting all hierarchical status in the context in which it properly belongs, namely at the foot of that crib, that martyr's wreath. We often speak of Christ as a High Priest (e.g. Heb. 3:1), representing us before God. We may even occasionally deck him out in glorious robes, as a mighty prelate. But his whole life began and continued as a deacon, where he is a servant (a deacon) of all, and he calls us to be servants of each other (Mark 10:43). There is nothing necessarily liturgical about this ministry, for we note that the servants, deacons, were those who dealt with the wine at the wedding in Cana of Galilee (John 2:5,9). Bethlehem is God's back door into the human race, through which he sneaks into our midst, and spends much of his time unnoticed, ignored, or uncomfortably challenging. Stephen's closeness to Christmas is at heart a subversive celebration, which threatens our systems and our certainties, political, social, ecclesiastical.

Today's Collect is a revision of that contained in *The Alternative Service Book (1980)*. This is itself a considerable reworking of the 1662 Prayer Book, which is an expansion of that contained in the first Prayer Book, which is in turn a translation of the old Latin prayer – which originally didn't even mention Stephen by name! Such an unsettled tradition reflects a kind of unease with Stephen's story. Be that as it may, the new Collect tells the tale; Stephen prayed for the forgiveness of those who were stoning him, and we pray for that capacity to forgive as well, and also for the faith to look to heaven and see the crucified Christ. The narrative of Stephen's martyrdom is the invariable reading before the gospel (Acts 7:51–60). If there is to be an Old Testament reading, it is the stoning to death of Zechariah the son of Jehoiada (2 Chr. 24:20–2). If the Acts reading is read first and there is to be an epistle, we hear Paul's teaching about justification in Christ; it is no longer ourselves who live, but Christ in us (Gal. 2:16b–20). The medieval and Prayer Book gospel was Christ's warning about crucifixion and persecution (Matt. 23:34–9). The revisions of recent years have changed this to Christ's earlier warning, that the disciples should be wise as serpents yet innocent as doves, and that the Spirit will give them the words to speak when they are forced to give witness to Christ (Matt 10:17–22). This is probably a better reading, because it embraces the fact that Stephen himself was given boldness to make that lengthy speech in front of the Jews before his death. The Post-Communion Prayer is from *The Promise of His Glory* (1991), and is inspired by the new Roman rite for this day: '. . . the signs of your mercy revealed in birth and death are the bread and wine of the eucharistic food and the celebration of Christ's birth and Stephen's death'.

Among the many sermons preached by E. B. Pusey (1800–82), there is one which was delivered on this day. He reflects carefully on the narrative of Stephen's life and death in a sermon entitled 'The Character of Christian Rebuke'. His words serve to mark the distance between our own faltering attempts to follow Christ and Stephen's dramatic end, without diminishing the cost of the martyrdom commemorated today:

In St Stephen every word and action breathes a divine might and holy awe, bearing down before him the opposition of man's rebellion . . .

He Who perfects His instruments in different ways would, by that very difference, teach them that their course, from first to last, is not of their own wisdom, but by His Guidance. He would prepare us to trust ourselves beforehand with Him, desiring nothing but what He appoints; wishing for nothing but patient, thankful hearts, to commit our way to Him; fearing nothing but to miss or fall short of His Gracious Will towards us; thankful for everything whereby He hinders us from following our own, and rivets us closer to His; glorying in nothing but that we are not our own, but His.

E. B. Pusey, *Parochial Sermons* (Oxford: Parker, 1852), Vol. I, p. 78.

John, Apostle and Evangelist
27 December (Festival – White)

When I was a teenager, I would often go and spend the weekend with an old priest who lived on the Isle of Cumbrae, in the River Clyde, at a town called Millport. He had been ordained before the First World War, and had served as a Chaplain in the trenches. He was that old-fashioned breed of scholar/priest that has served so faithfully both the Anglican and Lutheran traditions in the past, a man who was described by his bishop when he died as 'so rooted in reality that nothing seemed able to destroy him'. Looking back on those weekends and that long friendship, I may have learnt more theology from him than perhaps from anyone else. It was not that he set out to teach me, it was simply that our personalities clicked and beneath all the insults that we would trade in that extraordinary kitchen of his, wisdom kept being imparted in a seemingly effortless fashion, particularly late at night by his fireplace, as billows of the most revolting tobacco smoke came out of every aperture of his body.

On one occasion, we were talking about the four Gospel writers and the different ways in which they are depicted in the icon tradition of the East. 'You must always remember,' he said, 'that in addition to having an eagle above him, John is always dictating, whereas the other three evangelists are always writing.'

The eagle is the last of the four living creatures (Rev. 4:6f.) that we apply to the evangelists. John is the eagle, the powerful, far-seeing follower of Christ, the writer of the 'spiritual Gospel', in the words of Clement of Alexandria in the third century. He is frequently associated with – but might not be – the 'disciple whom Jesus loved', as he appears to describe himself repeatedly in the Fourth Gospel. But he dictates, as he looks away into the distance. Whereas the red of martyrdom is worn for the other three Gospel writers, white has always been reserved for John, not because we are near Christmas, but because according to a tradition he died in exile, on the Isle of Patmos.

He is regarded as the author of the Fourth Gospel and his name is also given to the book of Revelation, and to no fewer than three Epistles. All these authorships have been much discussed. It is not unreasonable to suppose that the Fourth Gospel stems from his work, and that the Revelation and the three Epistles are part of a 'Johannine' tradition. What this means is that there was a group of people who centred around John, his teaching and writing, and who developed it as time went on and circumstances and needs changed.

His Gospel, however, must be central to today's celebration. The tradition that he dictated, rather than wrote, distances him from the other three evangelists, because of his own particular style. Fashions in biblical scholarship change, and whereas a past generation seemed to drive a wedge between Matthew, Mark and Luke on the one hand, and John on the other, in recent years they have been brought nearer. Nonetheless, John does stand out with his own special characteristics. There are no infancy narratives such as we have noted in Matthew and Luke; and he does not begin with John the Baptist in the wilderness as in the case of Mark. Instead, John is 'topped and tailed' by a prologue (John 1:1–18) and by the lakeside appearance of the risen Christ (John 21:1–25). The prologue is the principal and traditional gospel for Christmas, which sets the Incarnation of the Word in cosmic and eternal dimensions. The concluding chapter, which may – like the prologue – have been added to an original earlier core, gives yet more appearances of Christ to the disciples, first in the fishing expedition, next in the lakeside breakfast, then in the charge to Peter to 'feed my sheep' and finally in Peter's questioning of Jesus about how John's discipleship will differ from his. This extra, final chapter ends with those memorable words, 'But there are also many other things which Jesus did; were every one of them to be written, I suppose that the world itself could not contain the books that would be written' (John 21:25).

John's Gospel, therefore, begins and ends in a way that suggests a history that will go on forever. Moreover, special features pervade the rest of the Gospel. There are not many miracles, but eight 'signs': water into wine at Cana in Galilee (John 2:1–12), the cleansing of the Temple (John 2:13–22), the healing of the official's son from a distance (John 4:43–54), the healing of the lame man on the Sabbath (John 5:2–16), the feeding of the five thousand (John 6: 1–15), walking on the water (John 6:16–21), the healing of the man born blind (John 9:1–41), and the raising of Lazarus (John 11:1–44). All these represent signs of the Kingdom of God, and they are increasingly surrounded by argument and by teaching.

When it comes to the Last Supper, there is no narrative of Christ's words, or his actions with the bread and the cup, only an allusion to the meal. Instead, he washes the feet of the disciples (John 13:1–20); and this is followed by even more teaching, commonly referred to as the 'farewell discourses' (John 14–16). A similar reticence surrounds his baptism. Whereas the other three Gospel writers all give us direct accounts, John gives a retrospective account by John the Baptist himself (John 1:32–4).

John's passion narrative is the richest of all, and it is traditionally read on Good Friday. John's account places Jesus in control throughout. He is a king – with a difference. Those who come to arrest him fall to the ground (John 18:6). In the judgement hall, Pilate is the prisoner, unable to make up his mind, and Jesus is the judge, answering his questions with counter-questions (John 18:33–8). Jesus carries his own cross to Calvary, going as one who has power to lay down his own life (cf. John 10:17–18). Just before he dies, he cries out that God's purpose is accomplished (John 19:30). Moreover, John dates

Christ's death to the Passover itself, whereas the other three
Gospel writers make the Last Supper the Passover meal. Thus,
Jesus is the 'Lamb of God, who takes away the sin of the world',
as John the Baptist himself had declared at the very beginning
(John 1:29), and Pilate delivers him to be crucified at the very
time when the lambs are being prepared for sacrifice (John
19:14). Yet Jesus is also the King, reigning from his tree in glory,
and this glory is what Christ prayed for the night before: 'I
glorified thee on earth, having accomplished the work which
thou gavest me to do; and now, Father, glorify thou me in thy
own presence with the glory which I had with me before the
world was made' (John 17:4–5). And just as no book on earth
can contain the words and deeds of Christ, so he forms the new
Easter community when he commends his mother to the disciple
whom he loved, and the disciple whom he loved to his mother
(John 19:26f.).

John and his brother James, as we have already seen, were
part of that 'inner cabinet' who in the other three Gospels shared
special moments with Jesus (see 25 July), and there are more
mentions of John in the New Testament than of any other
apostle, save Peter. In the Acts of the Apostles, he and Peter
went to the Temple together (Acts 3:1) and performed healing
(Acts 3:4f.). They refuse not to speak about Jesus (John 4:19)
and they go together to Samaria when the apostles learn that
the gospel has been accepted there (Acts 8:14). The Epistles that
bear John's name extend and develop the teaching of the Gospel,
and from exile in Patmos (Rev. 1:9) this John, or another writer
in the same tradition, has a vision that gives hope to a persecuted
Church, and sets the history of the Church in the context of a
cosmic struggle, at the end of which God's purposes are finally
made known.

John entered the calendar at an early stage, as clearly he had
to. The earlier custom in both East and West was to commemorate James and John as brothers together today, or else near each
other, but John settles on today on his own in Rome in the
mid-sixth century. Today's Collect goes back to the Prayer Book,

which is based on the Latin prayer as originally composed for the day. Its fourfold repetition of the image of light, so prominent in the Fourth Gospel, is the Prayer Book's device here, and eminently appropriate today. The Old Testament reading tells of Moses taking the tent and pitching it outside the camp, where he would consult with the Lord (Exod. 33:7–11a); this expresses both the mobility and the intimacy of God's presence with his people, now made all the more powerful in the Word made flesh, dwelling ('pitching his tent') among us, as we hear in the Christmas gospel (John 1:14). The epistle consists of the opening words of the first epistle of John – 'that which we have seen and heard we proclaim also to you, so that you may have fellowship with us' (1 John 1) – and was chosen for this day in the Prayer Book. The gospel, which has invariably been read today, is the final passage of the last chapter of the Gospel itself, where Jesus replies to Peter's question about John's discipleship, 'What is that to you? Follow me!' (John 21:19b–5). The Post-Communion Prayer is from *The Promise of His Glory* (1991), and is based on the Roman rite; may the word made flesh 'ever abide and live within us' in the sacrament and in discipleship.

In 1928, Kenneth Kirk (1886–1954) delivered his famous 'Bampton Lectures' at Oxford, which were subsequently published in a book entitled *The Vision of God*. This is how Kirk applies the Fourth Gospel to his quest for that vision:

> The vision is always a *corporate* one. 'We' is the word used throughout. This implies that the experience of the Church makes up for deficiencies on the part of the individual; even those who have *not* seen are blessed, the Fourth Gospel asserts, because they share in the Church's belief (John 20:29). It implies, further, that any alleged experience of the individual must be tested and overruled by this corporate vision of the Church ... Once more we come back to the cardinal belief that what matters, for the individual Christian, is not that he should have such and such 'experiences' here

and now; but that he should be standing in the right attitude towards God and the Christian fellowship.

Kenneth Kirk, *The Vision of God* (the Bampton Lectures for 1928) (London: Longmans, 1931), p. 108.

The Holy Innocents

28 December (Festival – Red)

When I was a University Chaplain, I came across a church dedicated to The Holy Innocents for the first time. One of the impressive features was that they made Holy Innocents' Day special! They resisted the temptation to let it go by the wayside in the post-Christmas haze. I remember on one occasion being asked to preach and I had an interesting time looking at the history of this celebration.

The story of the massacre of the infants is a special part of Matthew's infancy narrative, which invariably forms the gospel for today (Matt. 2:13–18). The wise men have departed without returning to King Herod. Once again, an angel appears to Joseph in a dream, and he is bidden to take Jesus and Mary to Egypt and remain there. Herod, unaware of the young family's escape, but angry that the wise men had not returned to him, has every single male child under two years old in Bethlehem killed. The pundits tell us that perhaps there could only have been about twenty children in that category at the time, but legend has exaggerated that number to 14,000. And so Holy Innocents became an occasion to commemorate all infant victims of famine, thirst, the sword, or cold.

It is Matthew's intention to use this part of his narrative in order to bring an atmosphere of danger into Christ's life from the very beginning. In Luke's case, it was the long journey from Galilee to Bethlehem for the imperial census (Luke 2:1–7), and Simeon's second oracle to Mary in the Temple, that 'a sword will pierce through your own soul also' (Luke 2:35). Christ's birth must be recorded as an historical event, and his infancy must also include a flavour of his future life and death.

Today's feast originated in the East in the fourth century, and Peter Chrysologus, who was Archbishop of Ravenna in the fifth century, preached a sermon on this day. The Innocents have long fascinated artists and hymn-writers. Laurence Housman's famous hymn which begins with the words 'When Christ was born in Bethlehem' ends with these two verses:

> Your lips on earth that never spake,
>   Now sound the eternal word;
> And in the courts of love you make
>   Your children's voices heard.

> Lord Jesus Christ, eternal child,
>   Make thou our childhood thine;
> That we with these the meek and mild
>   May share the love divine.

(New English Hymnal, no. 203)

Fascination with the Innocents as tragic figures even led to a tradition in the Ethiopian Church that only the four living creatures (Rev. 4:6f.) could intercede for them, since none of the New Testament saints had yet died. In Constantinople the main Eucharist was celebrated in the church of Mary Theotokos (Godbearer) in Chalkoprateia, the copper market district: a sign of the importance that was given to the occasion. (All that is left of that church today is the old apse next to a modern cinema.) In late medieval England, black vestments were often worn, and muffled peals rang out from our steeples.

In any age, victims of famine, thirst, sword, or cold are people who get in the way, people who meet their end by circumstances outside their control. We do not need to look far in Christmas newspapers or the centres of our own cities to see them, young and old. Moreover, there is a subtle interchange in the drama of Christ being taken as an infant to Egypt in order to escape death, the very place where his ancestors suffered so greatly, and where Moses had miraculously escaped Pharaoh's cruel massacre of the firstborn sons (Exod. 2). Matthew, the very Jewish evangelist, implicitly compares Jesus with Moses, but the redemption that Jesus is about to bring through his life, teaching, death and resurrection is infinitely greater than Moses' almost miraculous survival as an infant, and his dogged persistence before the Egyptian authorities as he leads the people of Israel from Egypt into freedom (Exod. 12:1–14, 31).

The Innocents are indeed innocent, because they were the victims of Herod's self-absorption, his cruelty, his displaced vengeance. And although today's feast is out of synchrony with the Epiphany, when the wise men come to Bethlehem, it is appropriately close to Christmas, and follows on from the feasts of first martyr and the disciple whom Jesus loved. In fact, this may explain why the principal gospel reading on 25 December in the Greek Orthodox Churches and throughout the Byzantine rite is not Luke's narrative of the birth of Christ (Luke 2:1–15) but Matthew's narrative of Christ's birth and the wise men coming from the East (Matt. 2:1–12). It also brings home Jesus' own attitude to children, exemplified by Matthew himself later on, when the disciples ask Jesus, 'Who is the greatest in the kingdom of heaven?' Jesus calls a child, and after placing him in the midst of them says: 'Truly, I say to you, unless you turn and become like children, you will never enter the kingdom of heaven. Whoever humbles themselves like this child, he is the greatest in the kingdom of heaven. Whoever receives one such child in my name receives me; but whoever causes one of these little ones who believe in me to sin, it would be better for him to have a great millstone fastened round his neck and to be drowned in the depth of the sea' (Matt. 18:1–6). It is hard to read that passage without thinking of today's feast, and without being challenged about our attitudes to children.

Today's Collect is a revision of that contained in *The Alternative Service Book (1980)*, restoring some of the Collect in the 1662 Prayer Book; this in turn was a considerable reworking of the Latin Collect which had been translated and used in the

first Prayer Books of 1549 and 1552. It meditates appropriately
on suffering and innocence, and prays that God's 'reign of justice
and peace' may be established. The Old Testament reading is
the voice in Rama of Rachel weeping for her children (Jer. 31:
15–17), which Matthew himself quotes at the end of the Gospel
passage (Matt. 2:18). The medieval and Prayer Book epistle was
John's vision of the undefiled in the book of Revelation (Rev.
14:1–5), but this has been replaced by a short passage from the
opening of Paul's first letter to the Corinthians: God chooses
what is weak in the world to shame the strong (1 Cor. 1:26–
9); and the gospel is Matthew's narrative of the flight into Egypt
and the massacre of the Innocents (Matt. 2:8–18). The Post-
Communion Prayer is a new composition, which meditates on
the defenceless children and the commemoration of the passion
in the Eucharist. It is a verbal and sacramental reminder of the
liturgical colour of today, namely red.

Holy Innocents' Day brings us face to face with the unnecess-
ary cruelty that is part of our world. Herod was such a cruel
monarch, and so keen to be a successful flunky of the Roman
Emperor, that he had some of his own children killed in order
to make his throne secure, and certain politicians had to be
executed on his own death in order to ensure some genuine
mourning among the people. This is power abuse in its most
ruthless form.

This theme is explored by John V. Taylor:

> Yet ruthlessness is not the last word. It is not the Word that
> was made flesh at Bethlehem. That birth, and the life and
> death and resurrection which followed, provide the clue by
> which we can detect this other law at work in the processes
> of the universe, one which lies at a deeper level than the
> stimulus of rivalry and self-preservation. It is the law of self-
> oblation. Without that clue we might never have suspected
> its existence, but once it is pointed out to us we find evidence
> of it on every side. The pelican pecking its breast to feed its

young with its own blood may be only a myth but its use as a symbol of Christ shows how readily the church took it for granted that these 'lesser calvaries' could be found in the natural order ... we speak of turning points in history, but the living and dying of Jesus has, in fact, been the only one.

John V. Taylor, *The Go-Between God: The Holy Spirit and the Christian Mission* (London: SCM Press, 1972), pp. 34f.

Part Two: The Easter Cycle

Ash Wednesday

(Principal Holy Day – Violet or Lenten Array)

Lent is not a time to become as miserable as possible, yet that is its popular reputation and it is not difficult to see why. Memories come to the foreground of campaigns to give up chocolate or sugar for the season, and of devotional addresses – or Lenten study groups – with a great deal of soul-searching, much of it very constructive. One of my predecessors as Bishop of Portsmouth had the courage to impose a ban on diocesan meetings in Lent, in order to stop the Church being so busy. Lent thus draws to itself different moods.

These can be explored by three particular strands in the Christian story. One is the preparation of candidates for baptism at Easter, which was particularly strong in the fourth century, whether in the great centres like Jerusalem with figures such as Cyril, or in such out-of-the-way places as Verona, with a Bishop like Zeno.

Secondly, in the early centuries Lent became a season when those who were debarred from communion did penance. In the third century in North Africa, Tertullian tells us of a discipline – though he does not link it with Lent, which was yet to emerge – whereby certain people who had sinned gravely against the community had to prostrate themselves at the feet of the clergy and ask for the congregation's prayers for pardon.

The third strand is about preparing for Holy Week and Easter with a fast, and this would normally involve abstaining from food until the evening of each day. Fasting can be easily misunderstood – like the quaint practice of giving up something sweet, almost for the sake of it! Nor should fasting be confused

with dieting, which is the deliberate limiting of food in order to
lose weight. Fasting is to abstain, in order to appreciate the real
value (if any) of what one is depriving oneself. Fasting can have
the effect of focusing the mind, and when I was a University
Chaplain, I used to advise students not to eat much food just
before an exam, because their whole bodies would be on the
alert if deprived of the usual pattern of sustenance.

Thus the season of Lent has three particular aspects. The
first is about preparing for Easter baptism. The second is about
penitents and their reconciliation with the Church. And the third
is about fasting. The genius of Lent is about how everyone can
be drawn into those three patterns of discipleship.

The length of Lent has varied. It has not always been forty
days long, corresponding with Jesus' time in the wilderness as
narrated by Matthew and Luke (Matt. 4:1–11; Luke 4:1–13).
The modern scheme starts on Ash Wednesday, and ends on
Easter Eve, the forty days comprising the intervening weekdays,
since Sundays do not count! The liturgical colour for today
marks its own distinct shift. In the Middle Ages, it was often
the custom to use unbleached linen vestments and to cover bright
and elaborate decor with the same sackcloth-like material, called
the 'Lenten Array'. Violet is the commoner colour today.

But what about the ashes? The Old Testament has several
references to the use of ashes as a sign of penitence, and they
often went with either wearing a hairshirt or rending one's
clothes (Gen. 18:27; 2 Sam. 13:19; Job 2:8, 30:19, 42:6; Isa.
58:5; Jer. 6:26; Jonah 3:6). The ash was sprinkled over one's
head, as a personal response to sudden changes of circumstances.
In the New Testament, Jesus challenges Chorazin in Bethsaida
to repent (Matt. 11:21; Luke 10:13). But he warns against public
show in personal religion, for when we fast, we must not fast
like the hypocrites (Matt. 6:16–21 – the historic gospel reading
for today).

The early 'class' of penitents had ashes sprinkled over them,
but soon everyone else wanted to take part in this custom, and
to do so at the start of Lent, when they would hear in addition

Joel's call to 'rend your hearts and not your garments' as the first reading at the Eucharist (Joel 2:12–19). Today was often called either the 'beginning of the fast' or 'the day of the ashes', reflecting two of the three strands to Lent that we noted earlier. By the ninth century, blessing prayers started appearing in the Sacramentaries, at the same time as prayers to bless candles at the Presentation in the Temple (see 2 February) and the branches on Palm Sunday (see Palm Sunday). All these blessings and distributions, whether of ashes or candles or palms, took place before the Eucharist and they attracted additional ceremonies.

Today's Collect goes back to the Prayer Book. It stresses the penitential character of the day and the readiness of God to forgive and to renew. The historic readings for today (Joel 2:12–18; Matt. 6:16–21) have been expanded so that their contexts are clearer (Joel 2:1–2, 12–17; Matt. 6:1–6, 16–21). Alternatives are provided in the form of Isaiah's call for the right use of fasting (Isa. 58:1–12) and the woman caught in adultery (John 8:1–11). The epistle is invariably Paul's catalogue of suffering, 'as having nothing and yet possessing everything' (2 Cor. 5:20b–6:10). The Post-Communion Prayer roots Christ's sacrifice for sin in us as 'also an example of godly life'. This is a new use of the Prayer Book Collect for the Second Sunday after Easter, which gives to Ash Wednesday a resonance of Easter hope.

The custom of 'ashing', like processing with candles on 2 February and palms on Palm Sunday, was abolished at the Reformation, though the old name for the day remained. The revisions of recent years, including the Roman, now agree on placing the ashing after the liturgy of the word, so that this ceremony is given a liturgical grounding. Receiving ashes for Anglicans remains optional. It took me some years before I was able to go up and receive that mark on my forehead with a reminder of my mortality, 'remember that you are dust and to dust you will return . . .' (Gen. 3:19). Late medieval custom was to burn the branches used on Palm Sunday in the previous year in order to create the ashes for today, but this is not by any means necessary. The two traditional readings for today (Joel 2:12–18; Matt. 6:16–21) in any case are their own warning against a religion which is outward show and nothing more. It is perhaps worth noting that the Christian East has nothing of Ash Wednesday in its rich traditions.

An age like ours has recovered many old practices, and now relates more confidently to these symbolic actions. Ashes express the brokenness of nature, and their use in the liturgy points to God alone as the source of wholeness. In 1664 Simon Patrick (1626–1707), one of the devotional writers of his time, wrote *The Parable of the Pilgrim*. This work was unfortunately overshadowed by John Bunyan's *Pilgrim's Progress*, which appeared afterwards in 1678. Right at the end, Patrick's Pilgrim is given some sound advice about the character of his journey of faith, which is always about nurture, about penitence, and about abstinence of one kind or another, regardless of the outward form of one's religious observance:

> Faith cannot apprehend things otherwise than God has revealed them; it cannot receive the Son of God in any other manner than as the Father gave him . . . Let your faith be as large as the Gospel itself.

Alexander Taylor (ed.), *The Works of Simon Patrick* IV (Oxford: University Press, 1858), p. 387.

Palm Sunday

(Red)

I always looked forward to Palm Sunday during my nine years in Guildford. We had two churches only a matter of a few hundred yards apart, and we would start the service at St Mary's, which was the smaller of the two, and process up the High Street to Holy Trinity. The police were alerted about this curious religious custom, which always seemed to attract a certain amount of interest in any case. We were never rained off – though on one or two occasions it was a close-run thing! We would cram into St Mary's, palm crosses would be distributed to each person at the door, the palms would be blessed, one of the narratives of Christ's entry into Jerusalem would be read, and up to Holy Trinity we would go, singing 'All glory, laud and honour to Thee, Redeemer, King' for as long as it took for everyone to find their places in Holy Trinity. One of the passion narratives would be read dramatically and the Eucharist would proceed, tailing off at the end into Isaac Watts' hymn, 'When I survey the wondrous cross', which was originally written for the Eucharist.

The service always managed to combine both triumph and tragedy. From the moment that we entered Holy Trinity, the mood would change. Different groups in the parish were directly involved in the service, from the willing gang who came to the Rectory a few weeks before for the making of the palm crosses, to the drama groups who would rehearse, and use different places in the church for the passion narrative. As a boy, I was always used to hearing Matthew's account of the entry into Jerusalem and of the passion (Matt. 21:1–11, 26:14–27:66), but the recent revisions have enriched that provision, to include the Marcan (Mark 11:1–11; 14:1–15:47) and the Lucan (Luke 19:28–40; 22:74–23:56) accounts. One of the fascinating exercises was to brief the drama group about the special characteristics of each of the passion narratives, which have already been noted in our discussion of the evangelists themselves (see 25 April, 21 September, 18 October, 27 December).

But where did Palm Sunday originate? It seems that the Sunday before Easter was often observed as a day of the Passion, which comes through in the practice in the West of reading one of the passion narratives on this day at the Eucharist. However, in Egeria's travel diary of her visit to Jerusalem between the years 381 and 386, we have our first glimpse of what was to become the later practice of the Palm procession. People would gather at 1.00 p.m. on the Mount of Olives for an extended afternoon service of readings and hymns, and then at 5.00 p.m. the Matthew narrative of the entry into Jerusalem was read and the bishop and all the people would start off on foot down the Mount of Olives and up to Jerusalem itself.

The liturgical trade route that we have already noted on many occasions so far whereby new customs start in Jerusalem and spread throughout the East and the West operated on this day as well. The Eastern rites – and the old Spanish rite – absorbed the palm celebration into the Eucharist. However, by the ninth century in the West, the custom arose of prefixing the Eucharist with a blessing and distribution of branches and the reading of the Matthew palm narrative (Matt. 21:1–11). The event gave rise to all kinds of local associations and in many large towns, it became the practice to start in one church and end in another – as we observed earlier in Guildford. This was in order to bring some dramatic colour into people's experiences of worship.

At the Reformation, the Palm Sunday procession was swept aside, along with the distribution of candles at Candlemas (see 2 February) and the ashing on Ash Wednesday (see Ash Wednesday). The Prayer Book calls this day 'The Sunday next before Easter', although the old nickname of 'Palm Sunday' persisted in popular usage. Anglican practice over the past century has seen a recovery of the older tradition of blessing the palms, and of reading the palm narrative before the main Eucharist. In the Byzantine rite, however, branches of palm or olive are now blessed and distributed at Matins, not the Eucharist.

Although the palm cross of recent centuries is popular in Anglican piety, the old medieval prayers are unspecific as to what kind of branch is blessed. In many Roman Catholic churches today, the older custom of blessing and distributing branches of any available tree has gained popularity. Are the palms blessed – or is it we who are to be blessed in our bearing of them? This question can also be posed in relation to candles on 2 February and ashes on Ash Wednesday! History's answer is a 'both and' – rather than an 'either/or'; candles are to enable our spiritual sight, the ashes to enable our inward penitence, and our bearing of the palms to enable us to walk more devoutly into the celebration of Holy Week. The palm *cross*, therefore, even though not very ancient, does provide an important focus on where Palm Sunday is going to lead, namely into Holy Week. For Palm Sunday marks the start of what is still called in parts of the East, 'The Great Week'.

Today's Collect is based on the Prayer Book, which in turn goes back to the Gregorian Sacramentary. In addition to the Palm and Passion gospel narratives from Matthew, Mark and Luke, there is also provision to read John's account as an alternative in the year when Mark is read (John 12:12–16). The Old Testament reading, which used to be read as the lesson for the epistle on the Monday of Holy Week, portrays the one who gave his back to smiters (Isa. 50:4–9a). The epistle is the hymn of the humility and exaltation of Christ (Phil. 2:5–11), which has been read on this day for centuries. The Post-Communion Prayer, taken from the Church of Ireland, is a noble meditation on humility and obedience in following Christ.

Evelyn Underhill (1875–1941) was one of the most remarkable writers of her generation. In 1936 she published a book entitled

– somewhat boldly – *Worship*. In it, she explores the nature of worship in the Bible and in the Christian tradition with original insights into different temperaments and traditions and liturgical experience:

> Jesus therefore taught worship by disclosing in His own person the true place of the soul of man in that current of eternal love which sets out from God and returns to God; and the cost and splendour of that destiny. But the long meditation and practice of devoted men and women were needed before all the implications of this destiny could be realised and expressed. The total adoring life of the whole Body, the Communion of Saints, is already present in His unconditioned response to the Father, His offering of Pure Love; and the history of Christian worship consists in its explication.

Evelyn Underhill, *Worship* (London: Nisbet, 1936), p. 223.

Maundy Thursday

(Principal Holy Day – White)

One of the recurring themes in our observations so far has been the particularity of Christian celebrations. As I write these words, Portsmouth Cathedral is preparing for the visit of Her Majesty the Queen for the Royal Maundy Service on the Thursday before Easter. It will be a spectacular occasion, as our cathedral is packed to the doors with a congregation that includes seventy-two men and seventy-two women (the age of the sovereign) who will receive coins specially minted for the occasion. Following in the footsteps of her ancestors, she is marking this day by making a public symbolic action of her service to her people as their monarch. Could the Queen arriving at the cathedral with her maundy money be an echo of the wise men bearing gifts?

The coins are not the original symbol of the occasion at all. Anglo-Saxon kings imitated the example of Christ and washed the feet of some few chosen subjects, as Jesus did after the Last Supper (John 13:1–20). There are those who would argue that this is what should really be done. Symbolic actions can, indeed, be interpreted in many different ways. The service in question, for all the grandeur and protocol surrounding it, will doubtless convey an intimacy and a warmth between the Queen and each one of those old people that they will never forget.

Maundy comes from the Latin 'mandatum', Christ's mandate, his command that we should love one another. It is a name given to today which is directly inspired by the foot-washing. This became a prominent part of today's observances in the Middle Ages in both East and West, in order to demonstrate that at the heart of the gospel we have to face the glory and the status of the world turned upside down. That is why later on the same day, I shall preside at the Evening Eucharist in Portsmouth Cathedral, and in the course of that celebration remove my outer liturgical garments (cf. John 13:4) and hobble around on the floor, all six feet three and a half inches of me, moving from one person to another, in order to wash the feet of twelve people seated before me for all to see. I do not expect it to change my personality, but the simple fact of repeating this action will have its own simple but profound effect on all who are present. Christ speaks in a way that is beyond words, and breaks through the formality and the context of the occasion in order to show us something of the meaning of the Kingdom he came to proclaim. For here we see Christ as an example of humility, in the fact that *he* washes *our* feet; Christ is the sanctifier of our weakness and sinfulness (he washes and cleanses); and he goes further, he washes the feet that will take his good news to the ends of the earth. Here is an acted parable that inspired a Benedictine monk in Reichenau around the year 800 to write a hymn ('Ubi caritas'), known in modern versions, to be sung during this ceremony:

Where charity and love are found, there is God.
    The love of Christ has gathered us together into one.
Let us rejoice and be glad in him,
        Let us fear and love the living God,
And love each other from the depths of our heart.
    Where charity and love are found, there is God.

What of today's Eucharist? Strangely, to celebrate the Eucharist in commemoration of the Last Supper on this day does not appear to have been immediately obvious to the early Christians. Egeria, for example, in her diary of the customs that she observed in Jerusalem during her visit there between 381 and 386, makes no mention of a Eucharist on this day either at the time or the place associated with the original meal. Perhaps this was because the passion of Christ was central, or because they believed that the Eucharist gathered into itself Last Supper, Good Friday and Easter Day on every single occasion that it was celebrated. In North Africa at the end of the fourth century, Augustine mentions a celebration both in the morning and the late afternoon, but he does not seem entirely happy with the latter, because of the importance of fasting before receiving communion. For us who live in an age when evening Eucharists are frequent occurrences, it sometimes appears baffling to face the more austere habits of antiquity.

Like other special ceremonies of Holy Week the foot-washing appears to have originated in the East, in Jerusalem, but it took place after the Eucharist. However, in most places in the medieval West, it tended to be carried out in monasteries and cathedrals only, where there were many clergy and a community in which this kind of ceremony was appropriate. Instead, the custom of taking the reserved sacrament to a side altar for the distribution of communion the next day took over as the focal point at the end of the Eucharist in the Roman rite, since the Eucharist was never celebrated on Good Friday.

The Reformation swept these practices away. The first Prayer Books call this day 'Thursday before Easter', contrasting with the Latin title, 'the supper of the Lord'. They do not even provide a proper Collect, the Passiontide prayer on Palm Sunday being regarded as sufficient. The epistle is an extended version of Paul's account of the Last Supper, with its warnings about due preparation and reverence (1 Cor. 11:17–34), and the gospel is Luke's account of the passion (Luke 23:1–49). This makes for a strong passiontide flavour. But another reason for this choice may well be the extended character of Luke's Last Supper scene, when compared with Matthew and Mark, with its even stronger accent on the *cost* of discipleship, as witness the dispute among the disciples about who is the greatest, and Jesus' challenging response (Luke 22:24ff.)

The recent revisions, however, have shown adjustments. Roman Catholics have simplified their practice, and Anglicans (and others) have learned to trust the older traditions more, by adaptation. The foot-washing now takes place (if at all) after the gospel narrative of that very scene (John 13:1–17, 31b–35) and this is preceded by the narrative of the Passover meal in Exodus (Exod. 12:1–4, [5–10], 11–14) and the central part of Paul's account of the Last Supper (1 Cor. 11:23–6). The Collect for today is a new composition written for *Lent, Holy Week and Easter* (1986) which expresses the atmosphere of this Eucharist, a commemoration of the death of the Lord until he comes (cf. 1 Cor. 11:26) and a prayer for nourishment and unity.

The Post-Communion Prayer, on the other hand, is an adaptation of the Collect written by Thomas Aquinas in 1264 for the Feast of Corpus Christi, which was a new feast to focus on thanksgiving for the institution of the Holy Communion on the Thursday after Trinity Sunday. This was in effect an extension of Maundy Thursday itself, but in an atmosphere free from the sombre mood of Holy Week. The prayer similarly looks back on the eucharistic memorial, and prays for reverence, spiritual growth and renewed discipleship.

I have always believed that however and wherever the Eucharist of the Last Supper is celebrated today, it has its own atmosphere that words cannot express, rather like the foot-washing itself. But there is one additional dimension that can easily be overlooked; a few chapters on from the foot-washing, Jesus is offering himself to the Father and praying for the *unity* of his followers (John 17:20). In a century that has seen a measure of friendship and agreement between separated Christians that would have been unthinkable in years gone by, this prayer for unity must neither be overlooked nor forgotten. For many Christians today are aware of differences which are often more to do with emphasis than substance. Whilst it can sometimes be quite painful to accept the reality of what continues to keep many of us apart, we nonetheless see the cross invisibly imprinted on the altar today, beckoning the whole world to the Saviour himself. For Maundy Thursday always needs to be seen in relation to the days which follow – to Good Friday and Easter morning. This is why the time between this Thursday evening and Easter morning has long been called the *Triduum Sacrum*, the 'sacred three days', to show how they form a unity in themselves.

Other associations with today, like the blessing of the oils in our cathedrals, are essentially secondary. This particular service has its origin in the need to make ready the oils used for the Easter Vigil baptism. Since such blessing is traditionally restricted to the bishop, and because the evening Eucharist of the Last Supper is rich enough on its own, another celebration began to be celebrated, and the blessing of the oil for anointing the sick was included alongside the oil used before baptism and the sweet-smelling oil of 'chrism' at confirmation. After the Second Vatican Council, a renewal of priestly vows was introduced in the Roman rite, which some regard as an intrusion. In order to safeguard the priority of the evening Eucharist, and the integrity of the 'sacred three days', this particular service is often celebrated earlier in the week, or on another occasion altogether. It has a long and venerable history, and it has much to commend it in its words and actions to the wider ministry of healing, as well as baptism and confirmation preparation and follow-up which are becoming increasingly common in our churches.

In 1881, W. H. Turton (1856–1938) wrote a hymn which began, 'O thou, who at thy Eucharist didst pray that all thy Church might be for ever one . . .' Its moving second verse leaves every eucharistic celebration on Maundy Thursday, however beautiful, as partially incomplete – and necessarily so:

> For all thy Church, O Lord, we intercede;
>   Make thou our sad divisions soon to cease;
> Draw us the nearer each to each, we plead,
>   By drawing all to thee, O Prince of Peace;
> Thus may we all one Bread, one Body be,
>   Through this blest Sacrament of unity.

Maurice Frost (ed.), *Historical Companion to Hymns Ancient and Modern* (London: Clowes, 1962), no. 403.

Good Friday

(Principal Holy Day – Red)

Early one summer in the late 1970s, the BBC descended on the old town of Boston in Lincolnshire to prepare for a broadcast of the television programme, 'Songs of Praise'. Among the people interviewed for their favourite choice of hymn was an old man who used to set up the market stalls and put them down again every Saturday. Everyone in Boston and in the surrounding villages knew him and he was what another generation would have described as 'a bit of a character'. His religion was old-fashioned and simple, and it had both directness and an agreeable measure of sentiment. When he was asked what his favourite hymn was, he replied straight off, 'The Old Rugged Cross'. The opening verse and refrain are as follows:

> On a hill far away stood an old rugged cross,
>   The emblem of suffering and shame;
> And I love that old cross where the dearest and best
>   For a world of lost sinners was slain.

> So I'll cherish the old rugged cross
>   Till my trophies at last I lay down;
> I will cling to the old rugged cross
>   And exchange it some day for a crown.

It is not common for a hymn's words and music to be written by the same person, in this case by George Bennard (1873–1958). But here is a clear example of a deep attachment to simple, biblical images, sung to a tune that is not without its sentimental side, which never failed to meet its mark on those occasions when families requested it at funerals. Light years away from many of the slick, correct, theologically balanced and well thought out revised liturgies of today, this hymn stands as a kind of off-stage personal aspiration of what the Saviour *has* done for me, and what I hope he *will* do for me in eternity. Those who plan special services do well to take care not to travel too far from this area of religious experience – and not least on Good Friday itself.

Good Friday is the medieval nickname for the day when the Church commemorates the crucifixion of Christ. It is the title that appears in the Prayer Book and no doubt it was used for centuries beforehand. It is the unique Friday of the whole year when the cross looms great and large. In Denmark, it is called 'Long Friday' – presumably because of the length of the passion narrative, and the three hours through which Christ hung on the cross. This day is both good and long because the salvation wrought here on Calvary puts the human race in its place, and shows it both the human and the divine consequences of this better way of living that Christ comes to show us.

We do not know when the Friday before Easter was first kept to commemorate the crucifixion. In her account of Jerusalem practices during her visit there between the years 381 and 386, Egeria tells us of an unfamiliar procedure, as unfamiliar to her as was the procession down the Mount of Olives on Palm Sunday. All morning 'the holy wood of the cross' (a relic of the true cross) is taken out of its gold and silver box and placed on a table with a cloth over it, while deacons stand around and guard it and the bishop sits in a chair behind. All the people come forward; 'they stoop down over it, kiss the Wood and move on'. Here is adoration of the crucified Lord in momentary form, and walking away, as it were, from Golgotha itself, in silent thought.

The liturgical trade route that we have already noticed on other occasions operated on Good Friday as well. Whether or not every single relic of the cross that circulated in the Middle

Ages was authentic is neither here nor there. But we encounter what was later called the veneration of the cross in Rome in the seventh century and it has remained part of the Roman rite ever since. Since Good Friday has never had a Eucharist in either Catholic or Orthodox traditions, the veneration of the cross was tacked on to the end of the service of the Word and prayers for this day, thus giving it an even more special character; and communion from the reserved sacrament, consecrated on the day before, was made available for those who wished it.

As the Middle Ages progressed, this service became increasingly elaborate, especially in monastic and cathedral churches. The passion narrative was chanted dramatically, the terrible and challenging 'reproaches' ('My people, what have I done to you?' – inspired by Micah 6:1–8) were introduced from northern Europe, with their elaborate chant, and 'creeping to the cross' (as it was known in England) became increasingly formalized, with three genuflections. Add to that an increasingly complex procession to and from the side altar for the sacrament, and the fact that only the celebrant received it, and you have a recipe for a severe Reformation. Sure enough, the Prayer Book reacts by reduction. It provides the Collect still used today, which goes right back to the Gregorian Sacramentary. To this was added two prayers inspired by the Intercessions from later on in the old Good Friday liturgy, first for the Church, and secondly for the Jews – always a sensitive subject today, not least from the anti-semitic climate of the late Middle Ages. Instead of the traditional reading of the Passover (Exod. 12:1–11), there is a long reading from the letter to the Hebrews about the eternal nature of Christ's offering of himself (Heb. 10:1–25). The John passion narrative (John 18:1–19:42) in the first two Prayer Books was reduced in 1662 to the central portion only (John 19:1–37).

Present practice reproduces a variant of this pattern. The Collect remains. In common with other revisions, including the Roman Catholic, the Old Testament reading is the 'Suffering Servant' of Isaiah (Isa. 52:13–53:12), eminently suitable for today. The epistle is either the second part of the Prayer Book reading (Heb. 10:16–25) or Christ the High Priest, who is able to sympathize with our weaknesses, and who offered up prayers with loud cries and tears (Heb. 4:14–16; 5:7–9). The gospel is the John passion narrative (John 18:1–19:42), which is the longest and possibly the most triumphant.

In many Anglican churches, the practice of venerating the cross and of offering extended prayers in a liturgical form has been introduced. This is in line with the (corresponding) simplification of today's liturgy that has been effected by the Roman Catholic church through the influence of liturgical scholarship and a better knowledge of the origin and development of these ceremonies. On the other hand, there are churches where the 'Three Hours' Devotion' is still popular in one form or another. This often consists of seven sermons on the traditional 'Seven Words from the Cross', uttered by Jesus, with hymns and prayers. It was instituted by Jesuits in Lima in 1687 after an earthquake. In other churches, there is often something akin to the three hours from 12.00 noon to 2.00 p.m., the last hour being taken up with an adapted form of the Good Friday liturgy.

There is also the question of whether to receive communion or not on this day. *Lent, Holy Week and Easter* (1986) in true Anglican style allows the options of ending the service without communion, distributing communion with elements consecrated the night before, or celebrating the Eucharist in full. Customs and preferences will inevitably vary, and there is a strand of Reformation piety, for example in German Lutheranism, that has celebrated the Eucharist on Good Friday. My own preference, for what it is worth, is that today's service appropriately ends without the sacrament, thus turning Good Friday, in all its 'goodness' and 'length', into a day of sacramental fasting. This was – and remains – the practice throughout the Eastern churches and also at Milan.

But whatever form the liturgy takes, the cross is so central in all its beauty and horror that, whatever form of service is used today, that truth must not be obscured. Perhaps it is thoughts such as these that lie behind the following words of Stephen Sykes (1939-):

> In the external forum it is *the* sacrifice – holy, costly, complete, efficacious. It deals with sin, because it concentrates evil publicly and openly – but is not obliterated by it. It deals with the ambiguities of power, because the sheer destructive energy of malevolence and weakness proves less powerful than goodness, humility and love.
>
> But it also has an unmistakable internal dimension, which we do not see – though we see its effects. For all who know themselves loved and befriended, even as co-crucifiers, there is a release from fear and impotence and casual malice. That is salvation.

Stephen Sykes, *The Story of Atonement* (London: Darton, Longman & Todd, 1997), p. 158.

Easter Day

(Principal Feast – White or Gold)

When I was a boy we spent the morning of Easter Eve – a Saturday – preparing our church for Easter. Flowers would appear from everywhere, mainly daffodils, tulips if we were lucky, and lilies. One of the tasks that I particularly enjoyed was helping to build the Easter Garden. This consisted of stones that fitted together into a cave, some figures representing Mary Magdalene and the Risen Christ (John 20:11–18) and the linen cloths lying inside the tomb (John 20:1–10). Moss was gathered from the Rectory garden each year and the ensemble gave to the onlooker a picture of Easter morning, made up of the natural and supernatural.

For nearly two thousand years, people have wrestled with what actually happened at that first Easter. For of all the feasts and festivals that we have so far looked at, this particular one is the hardest and deepest. We have looked at a select number of saints, those who accompanied Jesus or who were known – if only by tradition – to have been affected directly by his life. Added to these we have the powers of heaven, in the form of Michael and all Angels (29 September), and the all-embracing festival of All Saints (1 November). Then there have been the principal occasions of the liturgical year, culminating now in Ash Wednesday and Holy Week, and soon to be further unfolded in Ascension, Pentecost and Trinity Sunday. They all appear easy by comparison. Most of them rely on one particular narrative in the New Testament, although they may be supported by others in less detail here and there. But even in making that simple Easter Garden, we have not begun to fathom the 'unsearchable riches of Christ' (Eph. 3:8).

The Easter Garden brings us face to face with the gospel narrative that has tended to be read at the principal Easter Eucharist for centuries, namely Mary Magdalene coming to the tomb, the apostles Peter and John gazing inside and then going away (John 20:1–10); and it is sometimes followed by Christ's revelation of himself to her (John 20:11–18). But there are other Easter narratives. There are the two Marys coming to the tomb and being told by the anonymous young man that the crucified Jesus of Nazareth has risen, and they must tell the disciples and go on to Galilee – and their terror (Mark 16:1–8). There are the further appearances narrated by John of Jesus in the Upper Room, giving peace and the gift of the Holy Spirit (John 20:19–25); the appearance to Thomas (see 3 July); and the lakeside appearances at the fishing expedition, the breakfast, the questioning and charge to Peter, and the dialogue between Peter and Jesus about 'the disciple Jesus loved' (John 21). And there is also Luke's unique account of the walk to Emmaus, in which two hitherto unknown disciples are so intent in grief and bewilderment, that the unknown stranger is only – and fleetingly – recognized when, after unlocking the meaning of the scriptures, he is about to break bread with them (Luke 24:13–35).

These are but summaries, summaries that have provided sustenance for artists, poets, and preachers across the centuries. There is part of me that always dreads preaching on Easter Day, but another part of me which leaps to the challenge, because whether or not the outcome has much about it, at least I am trying to wrestle with that empty tomb, those appearances, that bewilderment and terror, and that strange companionship on the journey towards the eucharistic meal.

Easter cannot be locked up into a mere episode in the Church year as if it were a kind of heavenly soap opera. Easter is the earliest festival of all, and the early Christians seem to have begun their first halting attempts at liturgical celebration by keeping the death and resurrection of Christ in one fell swoop. For them Good Friday and Easter Day were one, as the full sweep of the passion narratives – each of which leads relentlessly on to Easter morning – makes clear in each case. This is why the Easter Vigil stands out in the history of Christian worship as so ancient and so eloquent in a way that natural historians would describe as 'arrested evolution'. It is a service that stopped developing quite early on, because it carried out its task adequately. For in the sharing of light, and the reading of the Old Testament, leading into the New Testament narratives, the Church rejoiced each year in that turning from the darkness of death into the light of Easter morning; and it began (from the third century onwards) to baptize new Christians *then*, and only having gone through such a rich and lengthy pattern of worship, to celebrate the Easter Eucharist.

Subsequent development formalized the sharing of candles, in antiquity a necessity at night-time. Although the great fourth-century preachers such as Cyril of Jerusalem and Augustine of Hippo made much of Easter baptism, the Church in general was never entirely convinced about such an exclusive focus. As the early Middle Ages progressed, this long service was anticipated, first into the afternoon of Easter Eve, and then on Easter Eve in the morning. It was probably only celebrated in monasteries and cathedrals where there were the resources. It had ceased to be important, and it was relegated to the margins, until recent times. The Easter morning Eucharist could stand on its own, with no special ceremonies other than a decorated church and joyous singing which provided sufficient sustenance.

In the Prayer Book, the Collect simply translates the Latin prayer in the Gregorian Sacramentary, and the epistle and gospel are those from Easter morning, namely Paul exhorting the risen community to 'seek those things which are above' (Col. 3:1–7) and, for the gospel, Mary and Peter and John at the tomb (John 20:1–10). The other narratives, together with testimonies to the resurrection from speeches of Peter and Paul (Acts 10:34–43, 13:26–41) are appointed to be read on Easter Monday and Tuesday, and similarly on the Sunday following. This makes the important point that Easter is a *season*, which is why recent revisions tend to shun the older tradition of speaking of Sundays 'after' Easter, and instead prefer to speak of Sundays 'of' Easter. Such a change is no liturgical pedantry. It is intended to enable the full breadth of the Easter narratives to speak out. When I was a parish priest, I was careful not to restrict Easter hymns to Easter Day itself, but to spread them out in such a way as to give their own background, colour and light to the readings of the particular Sunday.

Today's Collect is from *The Alternative Service Book (1980)*, and paints a dramatic picture of Christ's 'mighty resurrection' and the new life thereby imparted. In the alternative readings, there is a clear hint that if the Easter Vigil is celebrated, the epistle should always be Paul's image of the Christian dying and rising with Christ (Rom. 6:3–11) and the gospel should be read in sequence according to which year is observed in the lectionary (Matt. 28:1–10; Mark 16:1–8; Luke 24:1–12). It will also be noted that the Passover narrative must be read at the Vigil (Exod. 14:10–31, 15:20–1), but it is up to circumstances how many of the other readings should be used. This leaves the field open for the John narrative on Easter morning – and in its entirety (John 20:11–18), i.e. not just the empty tomb, but Christ's dialogue with Mary Magdalene. The Old Testament readings on Easter morning can be the building up of Israel by the Lord (Jer. 31:1–6), the vision of the heavenly feeding on the mountain (Isa. 25:6–9), or the new heavens and the new earth (Isa. 65:17–25); and all these may be replaced by Peter's witness to the resurrection (Acts 10:34–43). This reading may also be used instead of the epistle, where there is a choice between the old Latin Easter morning text which we have seen already (Col. 3:1–4), or one of two Pauline passages about the resurrection (1 Cor. 15:1–11 or 1 Cor. 15:19–26).

In the face of such a multiplicity of choice – and there is a strong argument for a certain stability on this day – it is worth pondering that in the East, the second Eucharist of Easter in the Byzantine rite always has the full text of the prologue to John's Gospel (John 1:1-17). This is a prime example of a text in context; 'we beheld his glory ... full of grace and truth' (John

1:14) gazes on the cross, and nothing else. But whichever Gospel passage is chosen today, our task in going out from the Easter Eucharist is 'to die daily to sin, that we may evermore live with him in the joy of his risen life', as today's Post-Communion Prayer, taken from Anglican draft revisions in the 1920s, makes clear.

Holy Week tells the tale of three human reactions to Christ: 'Hosanna' on Palm Sunday, 'Crucify him' on Good Friday, and the 'Easter Alleluia', which pervades today's celebration – and beyond. These ambiguities remain, however, and God alone makes sense of them. In his book *Resurrection*, Rowan Williams (1950-) seeks to apply the quest of Easter Day to the daily life of faith:

> To speak of the resurrection is . . . to speak of one's own humanity as healed, renewed and restored, recentred – in God; and the problems of talking about this are thus the problems of describing where one stands and who one is. You cannot see your own face, except in a mirror; you cannot describe with satisfactory completeness and objectivity the new life of Grace without looking at the resurrection of Jesus. But 'the risen Jesus' only has clear content in relation to the life of grace as experienced now . . . Jesus' risenness and our risenness are visible only obliquely, only in relation to each other. And this means that they are really uttered and manifested only in a speech that belongs directly within that relationship, a speech that is an intrinsic part of the process of discovering myself, and the human future overall, in the presence of Jesus. This is a language of worship and of active discipleship, a language that is eucharistic . . .

Rowan Williams, *Resurrection: Interpreting the Easter Gospel* (London: Darton, Longman & Todd, 1982), pp. 120f.

Ascension Day

(Principal Feast – White or Gold)

There are not many sermons that I remember from my child-hood, but I remember once listening to an eloquent preacher on Ascension Day. All I remember about what he said is that it had three points – often a good way of lodging ideas in the memory. Christ is our High Priest, our Forerunner, and our King. Exactly how we work these ideas out can be left to the imagination. But the sheer repetition, which was not obtrusive or facile, is its own lesson in the need for some kind of sensible and structured use of time in relation to the mysteries of the Christian religion. Christ is indeed our great High Priest who has passed into the heavens (Heb. 4:14), where he represents us before God, which is what a priest is for. He is indeed our Forerunner (Heb. 6:20) – the only use of that word in the New Testament – because in the Ascension we see in dramatic form God the Father drawing the Son to himself and giving him what we ourselves one day hope to share. Christ is, also, our King, which is the central charge levelled against him in all narratives of Jesus' trial before Pilate (Matt. 27:11; Mark 15:2; Luke 23:13; John 18:33). And in John's account, Jesus asserts that his king-dom is not of this world (John 18:36). To call Christ a King on Ascension Day is at one and the same time to evoke the image of a triumphant coronation after the resurrection, and to look back to the crown of thorns of which today is the consequence.

But from where did Ascension Day emerge? It is at root another Lucan festival and shows the influence of Luke yet again on the calendar and the Christian year. Right at the beginning of the Acts of the Apostles, we are told that after forty days of appearances, the Risen Lord tells the apostles that the Holy Spirit will come upon them and that they are to be faithful disciples, after which he is taken up into heaven (Acts 1:1–9). It needs to be noted that whereas the Acts of the Apostles *begins* with the narrative of the Ascension, Luke's Gospel graphically *ends* with a similar account (Luke 24:44–53). Indeed, there is a case for saying that the Ascension is *exclusively* Lucan, because Matthew's ending has Jesus on a mountain instructing his followers to baptize and to make disciples of all nations (Matt 28:16–20); John has no narrative whatever of the Ascension, except for that hint to Mary Magdalene that she is not to touch him, for he has to ascend to his Father (John 20:17); and Mark has a brief version of the Ascension, but in his 'second ending' which many regard as a later addition (Mark 16:14–20).

We do not know when this festival of the fortieth day after Easter was first celebrated, but we come across it in the fourth century and Egeria met it in Jerusalem between 381 and 386. Today's Collect is based on the Prayer Book, which in turn is largely inspired by the Latin Prayer from the Gregorian Sacramentary. The gospel reading is, appropriately, invariably Luke's account (Luke 24:44–53). (This is a happy and fuller substitution of the old Latin and Prayer Book choice of the 'late' Marcan version, Mark 16:14–20.) The first reading should be Luke's narrative from the beginning of Acts (Acts 1:1–11), which has always been read on this day. The two work well together, as they combine the themes of worship and obedient discipleship. For the Old Testament reading, there is Daniel's vision of the Ancient of Days in heaven (Dan. 7:9–14) and for the epistle, a passage from the beginning of Ephesians where Christ is depicted as sitting at God's right hand in the heavenly places, 'far above all rule and authority and power and dominion' (Eph. 1:15–23). The Post-Communion Prayer, written by Charles McDonnell, in four pithy sentences sums up the Ascension Eucharist – our humanity is raised in Christ and we have been fed with the bread of heaven; nourished with such blessings, we ask to 'set our hearts in the heavenly places' (see Eph. 1:20).

Much contemporary writing tries to connect the Eucharist with all the central Christian mysteries. The Eucharist indeed commemorates the death and resurrection of Christ, and it is a feast which rejoices in the outpouring of the Spirit, as witness the way in which the Holy Spirit is now invoked in so many modern eucharistic prayers. The Eucharist, too, through the puny elements of bread and wine expresses the vulnerability of Christ in the crib, a favourite theme of preachers down the ages. But there is a tendency to neglect the essential connection between the Ascension and the Eucharist, a truth which is evoked with some panache by Daniel Brevint (1616–95), in an influential work on the Eucharist which was published in 1673, and which fed subsequent generations, including the brothers John and Charles Wesley:

Now since He is gone up to heaven, thence He sends down on earth the graces that spring continually both from his everlasting Sacrifice, and from the continual intercessions which attend it. So that it is in vain to say, who will go up into heaven? Since, either without ascending or descending, the sacred body of Jesus fills with atonement and blessing the remotest parts of this temple.

Daniel Brevint, *The Christian Sacrament and Sacrifice: By Way of Discourse, Meditation, and Prayer upon the Nature, Parts and Blessings of Holy Communion* (Oxford: Vincent, 1847), p. 38.

Pentecost

(Principal Feast – Red)

What are we supposed to call today? Is it Pentecost or Whitsun? We are caught between two names for an important occasion, which causes confusion – and perhaps a little irritation – to people who ought to be united on this of all days! Pentecost comes from the Greek word meaning 'fiftieth', which is the day when in Luke's account the Holy Spirit descended on the disciples who were gathered in Jerusalem to observe the Jewish 'Feast of Weeks' on the fiftieth day after the Passover (Acts 2:1). On this day in Jewish tradition, the firstfruits of the corn harvest were presented (Deut. 16:9) and the giving of the Law by Moses was commemorated. The Christian Pentecost, therefore, supersedes the old; and the firstfruits of harvest and the giving of the Law are brought together in the descent of the Holy Spirit on the disciples, yet one more Lucan narrative to provide another part of the framework of the calendar and Christian year (Acts 2:1–11).

Whitsunday, on the other hand, is another vernacular nickname. Its origins in England are not entirely clear. Either the 'white' refers to the white robes of those who were baptized on this day, or to the white vestments worn at the Eucharist in Salisbury and at York, which were two of the most influential liturgical centres in medieval England. Liturgical colours varied at that time: red was used in some places, and it is the standard colour today, as expressing the fire of the Spirit. The first Prayer Books invariably and exclusively called today 'Whitsunday', doubtless reflecting popular custom. But whichever name is used, and Pentecost has more worldwide supporters than

Whitsunday, today's celebration focuses on that outpouring of the Spirit which resulted from the work of Christ, from God's raising of him in order to accomplish fully his eternal purposes.

All Christian traditions which use a Church year are at one in having Luke's account near the start of the Acts of the Apostles of the descent of the Spirit (Acts 2:1–11). Here is a picture of representatives of the known inhabited world, from all over the Mediterranean, gathered together to celebrate a Pentecost that was transformed by the Spirit descending upon them like a wind and in tongues of fire, equipping each one of them to speak in their own language 'the mighty works of God'. It is a scene worth pondering. Each one knows their own language, but it is the Spirit that enables them to speak in that language about God. As these languages co-mingle, chaos seems to reign, and some say that they are drunk with wine – even though it is only 9.00 a.m. But this scene has to look forward to further events, missionary enterprises, a new life for a new community whose consequences we are living with now so many centuries later. The Holy Spirit comes from above, for the purposes of what might somewhat baldy be called Christian communication. It is not to create a babble but to create coherence. Pentecost is a reversal of the Tower of Babel (Gen. 11:1–9).

This scene has always been balanced by a gospel reading from John. In the Byzantine tradition, it comes from early on, where Jesus asks any who are thirsty to come to him to drink, and the subsequent conflict with the chief priests and Pharisees, followed by his teaching that he is the light of the world (John 7:37–8:12). Here is the work of Christ communicating in a context of religious conflict, and setting that confusion aright. In the West, however, the gospel passage was always taken from the centre of the so-called 'farewell discourses' after the Last Supper, where Jesus promises the Spirit of Truth, who will teach the disciples all things (John 14:15–31). Here is a scene somewhat different in texture from the rushing wind and the tongues of flame, a more sublime and less dramatic atmosphere, but one which is in all essentials the same. The Spirit will continue and complete the work of Jesus in doing the will of the Father. From the confusions and fears will come coherence and direction. Our humanity will carry on being human, and yet the Spirit will show us what to say and what to do.

Today's Collect is based on the Prayer Book, which once more translates the version in the Gregorian Sacramentary. There is at first sight a bewildering set of readings. The Acts narrative must be read, and in its fullest version (Acts 2:1–21). The other readings vary according to the year of the Lectionary. For the Old Testament reading, Moses gathering the seventy and giving them some of the Spirit of God (Num. 11:24–30) or Paul's description of the gifts of the Sprit (1 Cor. 12:3b-13) precedes a gospel reading from John, which is either Christ giving the Spirit in the Upper Room after the Resurrection (John 20:19–23) or the beginning of the Byzantine reading for today, about coming to Christ and drinking of the Spirit (John 7:37–9). Alternatively, the valley of the dry bones in Ezekiel's vision (Ezek. 37:1–14) or Paul's assertion that we have the firstfruits of the Spirit, and the Spirit helps us in our weakness (Rom. 8:22–7) precedes another gospel from John, the giving of the Spirit of Truth (John 15:26–7; 16:4b-15). Alternatively, the Tower of Babel (Gen. 11:1–9) or Paul calling his hearers to be led by the Spirit of God (Rom. 8:14–17) precedes yet another gospel from John, where Philip asks Jesus to show the disciples the Father and Jesus replies that they must believe in him and do his works (John 14:8–17, to which may be added 25–7). The Post-Communion Prayer, inspired by the Acts reading, rejoices in the fulfilment of the promises of Easter in the gifts of the Spirit, and asks 'that every tongue may tell of your glory'; it is adapted from the Canadian *Book of Alternative Services* (1985).

One of the movements of our time has seen a renewed interest in reflection on the work of the Spirit renewing people's lives and working in the *world*. A truly 'charismatic' movement is not an exclusively 'churchy' exercise, but is rather about seeing

God at work, preceding our footsteps as his disciples. Worship, moreover, needs to embrace within itself the *whole* of Christ's life, before it can embrace the whole of ours. Christopher Cocksworth (1959-) gathers these considerations together in the following words:

> The Spirit's work of transforming God's people is intrinsically related to the experience of worship. The Spirit is the one who enables us to worship because the Spirit brings us into fellowship with Christ and therefore with each other and with his Father. As we worship we enter into the movement of Christ's self-giving to the Father through the Spirit (Heb. 9:14), which was the cause of his glorification and his death, and into the movement of his receiving of life and power through the Spirit, which was the cause of his glorification in his birth and baptism . . . by glorifying God, we are glorified because we are becoming what we have been created to be.
>
> Christopher Cocksworth, *Holy, Holy, Holy: Worshipping the Trinitarian God* (London: Darton, Longman & Todd, 1997), pp. 145f.

Trinity Sunday

(Principal Feast – White or Gold)

For longer than I dare to remember, I have sat down at the beginning of a sermon and heard the preacher's opening words, 'In the name of the Father, and of the Son, and of the Holy Spirit, Amen.' I have used those words myself, and I know that they trip off the tongue as if they were no more than another way of saying hello or goodbye. In some ways Trinity Sunday can seem like a way of saying 'goodbye' to all the fun, the Christmas and Easter cycles with their times of preparation beforehand in Advent and Lent, and their times of reflection and further celebration afterwards, in Epiphany and Candlemas, and Ascension and Pentecost. All that lies ahead is the long green season that the Roman rite refers to as 'ordinary time', as if all that is left is basic fare, occasionally interrupted by a saint such as James the Great (25 July) or Luke (18 October).

However, there is method in the madness of the Christian language. The doctrine of the Trinity has indeed inspired lengthy tomes from great theologians, but that is only because it lies in the pages of the New Testament, lightly concealed, but constantly present. Towards the end of the Letter to the Ephesians, for example, the writer exhorts us to be filled with the Spirit, to sing and make melody to the Lord in our hearts, giving thanks to the Father, in the name of Our Lord Jesus Christ (Eph. 5:18–20). Writing to the Philippians, Paul states that Christians worship in the Spirit of God and boast of Christ (Phil. 3:3). Whether one takes the episodic approach of Luke that carefully portrays resurrection and ascension and giving the Spirit, or the more

synthetic and meditative tempo of the Fourth Gospel, where
Christ shows the Father to the disciples and promises the presence of the Spirit, there is a Trinitarian grammar emerging,
which gave rise to the great prayers, hymns and discourses that
are prayed and sung and written across the centuries.

But why? Because to speak of God as Father, Son and Spirit
is to insist that God is *one*, that he is shown in Jesus his Son,
and lives now in the power of the Spirit. Moreover, in Father,
Son and Spirit are to be seen a way of understanding the human
race as permanently and eternally intended for relationship one
with another, which can defy precise description but is still
so real and true as to have an inevitable coherence about it.
For each word, Father, Son, and Spirit, is essentially relational:
fatherhood implies sonship, sonship implies fatherhood,
spirit implies breath given to someone else. These are not
optional extras invented by theologians for other theologians to
read! Nor are they the 'in-talk' of a few religious zealots who
are determined to be different from the human race. They are
rather words taken from the experience of every human being,
and baptized with new significance, new meaning, new appli-
cation.

It took four centuries for Christians to work out some of this
terminology, and that innate genius of diversity which is part
of what it means to be human created misunderstandings and
differences of opinion. That story goes on. But the overall con-
sensus was that the Christian understanding of God as Trinity
was already grounded in *prayer*, and that prayer to the Father
through the Son in the Spirit was to be the foundation upon
which all worship should be based.

This genius for diversity has its own implications for today,
for as we have seen, throughout the Byzantine rite, the Sunday
after Pentecost is their All Saints' Day. In a sense, they do not
really need a Trinity Sunday, because the Trinity pervades so
much of their prayer and iconography. When Lancelot
Andrewes (1555–1626) preached before King James I at Whitsun in 1612, he considered the Baptism of Christ as a manifes-

tation of the Trinity – 'The Father in the voice, the Son in the flood, the Holy Ghost in the shape of a dove'. In doing so, he was looking to the Christian East in particular for inspiration (see the Baptism of Christ). The narratives of Christ's baptism (Luke 3:21–2; Matt. 3:13–17; Mark 1:9–11) have indeed inspired painters and preachers. The other 'iconographic' Trinitarian text is where the Lord appears to Abraham and Sarah in the form of three figures by the oaks at Mamre (Gen. 18:1–15); this has also inspired Eastern painters, most notably the famous icon of the three angels by Rublev. Both these passages tell of an *encounter* between God and the human race, and in the case of the baptism of Christ, particularly if the Lucan narrative is followed, when 'all the people' are present as well (Luke 3:21). It is perhaps a pity, therefore, that in the midst of such a variety of readings, neither of these texts is suggested for liturgical use today.

In the West we need Trinity Sunday rather more, since many of our approaches to religious experience have either been too generally about God, or far too specifically focused on the person of Jesus. This may be why the Church of England wisely decided to adhere to the Prayer Book's tradition of reckoning Sundays 'after Trinity', following later medieval English practice. As far as the history of Trinity Sunday is concerned, we owe a great deal to Alcuin of York (*c.* 732–804), who wrote a series of prayers for the Eucharist for specific occasions which began with the mass of the Trinity. It is his Collect which was translated into English in the first Prayer Book, and which is still used today. Whether or not he intended that the Sunday after Pentecost should celebrate the Trinity, that is what eventually happened, and in the centuries immediately after his death, these prayers – and suitable readings – began to appear on this day. Gradually it came to be kept as a feast in its own right, though not universally until as late as 1334, by which time it was well established in the north of Europe. The Prayer Book retained the feast, and the Collect as well as the two readings. These are first of all the door open in heaven, the four living creatures, and the vision of heavenly worship (Rev. 4:1–11), and for the gospel, Jesus and Nicodemus (John 3:1–15). Sadly, the first reading is now relegated to being an option in the second service for today.

But the new provisions are nonetheless rich, and they vary according to the three-year cycle. Isaiah's prophecy of the Spirit of the Lord working as instructed by him (Isa. 40:12–17, 27–31) is linked to the very end of Paul's second letter to the Corinthians, 'The grace of Our Lord Jesus Christ and the love of God and the fellowship of the Holy Spirit' (2 Cor. 13:11–13), often used in votive masses of the Trinity in the Roman rite; these lead into Christ's parting instructions at the end of Matthew's Gospel to baptize in the threefold name and to make disciples of all nations (Matt. 28:16–20). Alternatively, Isaiah's vision of the holiness of God in the Temple (Isa. 6:1–8) is linked to Paul's teaching about being led by the Spirit (Rom. 8:12–17); and these lead into Jesus and Nicodemus (John 3:1–17), the traditional gospel reading for this day. Yet again, the wisdom of God as his own creature in creation and instruction (Prov. 8:1–4, 22–31) is linked to Paul rejoicing in the access that we have to the grace of God through Christ, because God's love has been poured into our hearts through the Holy Spirit (Rom. 5:1–5): and this leads into Jesus' promise that the Spirit will lead us into all truth (John 16:12–15). The Post-Communion Prayer contrasts the abstract language of the Collect ('In the power of the divine majesty to worship the unity') by praying for the gift of faith, knowledge, and joy in the Lord: '. . . hold us firm in this faith, that we may know you in all your ways and evermore rejoice in your eternal glory . . .' This prayer is adapted from the Church of South India's *Book of Common Worship*.

The Trinity is neither a silence from discussion, nor a celebration of completion, for it will always lead into more ways of knowing God. The Trinity is to be prayed to, and read about in Scripture, but it is above all to be *sung*. In perhaps one of his greatest

compositions, Charles Wesley (1707–88) wrote the following
hymn, in praise of Father, Son and Holy Spirit, drawing heaven
and earth together into an eternal unity:

> Father, in whom we live,
>   In whom we are, and move,
> The glory, power and praise receive
>   Of thy creating love.
> Let all the angel throng
>   Give thanks to God on high;
> While earth repeats the joyful song,
>   And echoes to the sky.
>
> Incarnate Deity,
>   Let all the ransomed race
> Render in thanks their lives to thee,
>   For thy redeeming grace.
> The grace to sinners showed,
>   Ye heavenly choirs proclaim,
> And cry: 'Salvation to our God,
>   Salvation to the Lamb!'
>
> Spirit of holiness,
>   Let all thy saints adore
> Thy sacred energy, and bless
>   Thy heart-renewing power.
> Not angel tongues can tell,
>   Thy love's ecstatic height,
> The glorious joy unspeakable,
>   The beatific sight.
>
> Eternal, triune Lord!
>   Let all the hosts above,
> Let all the sons of earth, record
>   And dwell upon thy love.
> When heaven and earth are fled
>   Before thy glorious face,

Sing all the saints thy love has made
Thine everlasting praise.

Hymns and Psalms: A Methodist and
Ecumenical Hymn Book (London,
Methodist Publishing House, 1983, no. 4.)

Epilogue:
Christ the King

(Principal Holy Day – White or Red)

To worship with angels and archangels and the whole company of heaven is to dare to claim that heaven is the perspective from which the earth is seen whole. In the preceding pages, we have looked at some of the saints and the mysteries of the Christian faith, not just as individual entities but as part of that coherence, that wholeness. There have been many strands to this story, whether in geography (the trade route from fourth-century Jerusalem westwards), historical (those saints who don't seem to have appeared in the calendar until a bit later, for example in the eighth and ninth centuries), and theological (the Prayer Book's desire to prune in order to let what appeared to be essential stand out).

Some occasions, like the Presentation in the Temple, are so all-embracing that it is hard for the tradition to fix on one particular title. There are differences, too, of emphasis and interpretation: the East is enthusiastic about Andrew as the 'first called' apostle (John 1:40ff.), whereas the West has followed Rome's attachment to Andrew's meeting Jesus at the same time as his brother Peter (Matt. 4:18ff.). Moreover, the special ceremonies of Holy Week, namely the palms, the foot-washing and the veneration of the cross, go back to Jerusalem, whereas the candles of the Presentation in the Temple and the ashes of Ash Wednesday are thoroughly Western. Some festivals arrived early on the scene and form a basic core between East and West, where agreement on a particular date suggests antiquity. These include Epiphany, the Presentation in the Temple, the Annunciation and the Transfiguration, as well as Mark, the Birth of

John the Baptist, Peter and Paul, Mary Magdalene, Luke and Andrew. Others perhaps surprise us in the time they took to arrive, like Joseph, and the full splendour of All Saints' Day. Then there are occasions that seem to defy our logic, like the Annunciation interrupting Passiontide at Easter, and Stephen's martyrdom coming straight after Christmas. This shows that God's work of redemption in us is full of paradox, in which life and death, light and darkness, joy and suffering have to co-mingle in order to allow the sense and coherence that God intends for us to reach us.

Nothing is static in what we have so far seen. Feasts and holy days travel through their own self-authenticating journeys, whether from the Holy Land, or Rome, or France, or England; the process is never-ending. The calendar and the Church year are not a system. They are an organism, in which different parts emerge here and there and are suddenly of more significance to one age and less to another, as witness our society's concern over attitudes to children when commemorating Holy Innocents' Day. Nonetheless we are left where we are in history, touched continually by God's eternity, and as we ponder these saints and these mysteries, we are made constantly aware that we are in the presence of truths much larger than ourselves.

One clear example is the celebration known as Christ the King. It is something of an irony that this festival was celebrated for the first time throughout the Roman Catholic Church as recently as 1926, as political instability increased in Europe after the catastrophe of the First World War, and monarchies were increasingly insecure as a result. Until the liturgical changes following the Second Vatican Council, this festival was held on the last Sunday of October. However, the opportunity was taken to give it a new position, namely on the Sunday before Advent, thus heightening the sense of the approach of God's reign in Christ. Other modern revisions have followed suit, hence its appearance in the new provisions.

The Collect was originally composed for *The Alternative Service Book (1980)*, for the twentieth Sunday after Trinity, whose theme was 'the Christian hope'. It is a fine composition, which starts with Christ's ascension 'to the throne of heaven that he might rule over all things as Lord and King'; it goes on to pray that the Church may be kept 'in the unity of the Spirit and in the bond of peace', so that 'the whole created order' may be brought to worship at his feet. It is significant, to say the least, that Christ's kingship is not only over human beings, but 'the whole created order', four living creatures (Rev. 4:6ff.) and all.

The readings follow the three-year cycle. Year A starts with God searching for his sheep (Ezek. 34:11–16, 20–4) and continues with the vision of Christ at the right hand of God in the heavenly places (Eph. 1:15–23); the gospel is the 'Great Assize' when the Son of Man comes in judgement (Matt. 25:31–46). Year B, on the other hand, begins with Daniel's vision of the Ancient of Days being given dominion (Dan. 7:9–10, 13–14) and continues with another vision, of Christ coming on the clouds (Rev. 1:4b–8); the gospel is Jesus standing before Pilate, telling him that his kingdom is not of this world (John 18:33–7). Year C provides another flavour: shepherds who destroy God's people are to be judged (Jer. 23:1–6); God has delivered us from the powers of darkness and had transferred us to the kingdom of his Son (Col. 1:11–20); the kingdom is inaugurated by nothing less than the crucifixion of Jesus of Nazareth (Luke 23:33–43). The Post-Communion Prayer is the famous 'Stir-up' Collect for the last Sunday after Trinity in the Prayer Book; this is, in fact, an old Latin Collect with a strongly Advent flavour, which resonates with the coming of Advent itself, where all considerations of Christ as King properly lie.

At the beginning of a famous hymn, John Mason (*c*.1645–94) asked the question, 'How shall I sing that majesty/Which angels do admire?' After contemplating God's brightness and eternity, and his own dark and cold life by comparison, he ends on a note of supreme confidence:

How greater being, Lord, is thine,
Which doth all beings keep!
Thy knowledge is the only line
To sound so vast a deep.
Thou art a sea without a shore,
A sun without a sphere;
Thy time is now and evermore,
Thy place is everywhere.

(*New English Hymnal*, no. 373.)

Glossary of Terms

Apocrypha From a Greek word meaning 'the hidden things'. The biblical books which appear in the Greek version of the Old Testament but are not included in the Hebrew Bible, and are therefore excluded by many Jews. Roman Catholics recognize these books, but most Protestant leaders rejected their use at the Reformation. They have begun to appear in Anglican worship, but usually with an alternative from the Old Testament, where possible.

Bible readings There is normally a maximum of three of these at the Eucharist in current usage. The gospel reading is mandatory, because it takes us to the direct witness of the early Church to the mission and ministry of Christ. Normally an Old Testament and epistle reading precede on Sundays and special occasions; where, however, a reading from the Acts of the Apostles or Revelation is required, it can either come in place of the Old Testament (in which case an epistle reading can be read) or instead of the epistle (in which case an Old Testament reading is possible).

Byzantine rite Byzantium is the old name for Constantinople, given it in AD 330 by the Emperor Constantine himself. It was renamed Istanbul after its capture by the Turks in 1453. The churches which use the Byzantine rite include both those Orthodox Churches in communion with Constantinople (Greek, Russian, Bulgarian, Romanian, Serbian and other), and much smaller groups from those countries which are in communion with Rome; these are often referred to as 'Eastern Catholic' (a large group being Ukrainian).

Calendar The list of fixed commemorations observed throughout the year. In this book, this applies to all occasions, except the Baptism of Christ (which falls on the Sunday after Epiphany); and Ash Wednesday, Palm Sunday, Maundy Thursday, Good Friday, Easter Day, Ascension Day, Pentecost, Trinity Sunday, and Christ the King. The latter vary from year to year, and are therefore often referred to as belonging to the Liturgical Year.

Christmas Cycle That part of the liturgical year which centres on Christmas Day, working backwards into Advent, and forwards into Epiphany, and the Presentation of Christ in the Temple.

Collect A variable prayer which comes near the start of the Eucharist in the West, immediately before the Bible readings. On ordinary occasions the Collect does not necessarily relate to the readings, but on saints' days and special occasions it invariably does. At the English Reformation, the Collect was retained and adapted, thanks largely (but by no means exclusively) to the work of Archbishop Thomas Cranmer. There are significant editorial improvements on his work in the 1662 book, and the revised versions in use today retain many of their cadences, rendering them appropriate for devotional use.

Coptic The Coptic Church is one of the 'Oriental Orthodox Churches', which, like its Ethiopian neighbour, and the Armenian and Syrian Orthodox Churches, are not in communion with Constantinople. Their traditions go back a long time, and their influence on early Christianity is considerable.

Diaspora A word meaning 'dispersion', referring to the migrations of Jews following the deportations under the

Assyrians and Babylonians in the eighth and late sixth centuries BC. By the time of the early Christian Church, the Jewish diaspora reached many parts of the Mediterranean world, and often provided the first Christians with a mission base.

Easter Cycle The Easter Cycle is that part of the Church year which, being unfixed, centres around Easter, working backwards into Holy Week, Lent and Ash Wednesday, and forwards into Ascension, Pentecost, and Trinity Sunday.

Lectionary This word either means a book containing the selection of readings taken from the Bible for liturgical use, or else a list of references to books from the Bible which indicate where those readings are to be found. Anglican usage tends towards the latter meaning.

Patristic A word used to describe the period of the 'Early Fathers', meaning the first Christian centuries, often taken to end around the seventh or eighth century. It was the time when the Greek and Latin Fathers developed Christian life and worship, and it is therefore regarded as formative.

Post-Communion Prayer In the old Latin Sacramentaries, there were other variable prayers besides the Collect, but these were all set aside at the English Reformation. In recent years, however, this variable prayer after communion has been revived, but it is optional. Like the Collect, it is frequently an aid to devotion.

Prayer Book A name given to *The Book of Common Prayer* of the Church of England. The most important edition is that of 1662, issued after the accession of King Charles II. The first two Prayer Books of 1549 and 1552 show an earlier development in the immediate aftermath of the English Reformation. Other Anglican Provinces have issued their own prayer books and service books, particularly in recent years.

Roman rite Strictly speaking, originally the liturgical practice of the Church in Rome, but for long used of churches in the West which recognize the Pope. However, 'Non-Roman Western' rites include those parts of the West which are Roman Catholic, but which have been allowed to retain their own liturgical traditions, e.g. Milan.

Sacramentary A book of prayers for the use of the President at the celebration of the sacraments of the Church in the early medieval West, particularly in the Roman rite. The most influential was the Gregorian Sacramentary, associated with Pope Gregory the Great (590–604), who was responsible for codifying and gathering together prayers in common use in Rome at the time; this was subsequently expanded, as its influence spread across the Alps into what are now France and Germany.

Further Reading

Service Books

Exciting Holiness: Collects and Readings for the Festivals and Lesser Festivals of the Church of England, (Norwich: Canterbury Press Norwich, 1997).

Lent, Holy Week, Easter: Services and Prayers, (London: Church House Publishing, 1986).

The Promise of His Glory: Services for the season from All Saints to Candlemas, (London: Church House Publishing/Mowbrays, 1991).

Other Works

John F. Baldovin, SJ, *The Urban Character of Christian Worship: The Origins, Development and Meaning of Stational Liturgy*, Orientalia Christiana Analecta 228 (Rome: Pontifical Institute of Oriental Studies, 1987).
A detailed study of the interaction of architecture, the calendar, and the liturgical year in the three ancient Christian cities.

F. L. Cross and E. A. Livingstone (eds.), *The Oxford Dictionary of the Christian Church* (Oxford: Oxford University Press, 1997).

G. J. Cuming, *A History of Anglican Liturgy*, second ed. (London: Macmillan, 1982).
A scholarly account of the Anglican story.

David Farmer, *The Oxford Dictionary of Saints* (Oxford: Oxford University Press, 1997).

Pierre Journel, *Le renouveau du culte des Saints dans la liturgie romaine*, Bibliotheca 'Ephemerides Liturgicae' Subsidia 36 (Roma: Edizioni liturgiche, 1986).
An historical description of the new calendar of the Roman Catholic

Church by a scholar closely associated with the work, who was also a personal adviser to Pope Paul VI.

Michael Perham, *The Communion of Saints*, Alcuin Club Collections 62 (London: SPCK, 1980).

Kenneth Stevenson, *Jerusalem Revisited: The Liturgical Meaning of Holy Week* (Washington: Pastoral Press, 1988).
A theological and historical account of the ceremonies of Holy Week.

Thomas J. Talley, *The Origins of the Liturgical Year* (New York: Pueblo, 1986).
A detailed study of the origins of Easter, Christmas, and Epiphany.

Index

John / Fourth Gospel

Alternative Service Book